C-3578

THIS IS YOUR **PASSBOOK**® FOR ...

SECRETARY II

NATIONAL LEARNING CORPORATION®
passbooks.com

COPYRIGHT NOTICE

Copyright © 2020 by

N L C ®

National Learning Corporation

212 Michael Drive, Syosset, NY 11791
(516) 921-8888 • www.passbooks.com
E-mail: info@passbooks.com

PUBLISHED IN THE UNITED STATES OF AMERICA

PASSBOOK® SERIES

THE *PASSBOOK® SERIES* has been created to prepare applicants and candidates for the ultimate academic battlefield – the examination room.

At some time in our lives, each and every one of us may be required to take an examination – for validation, matriculation, admission, qualification, registration, certification, or licensure.

Based on the assumption that every applicant or candidate has met the basic formal educational standards, has taken the required number of courses, and read the necessary texts, the *PASSBOOK® SERIES* furnishes the one special preparation which may assure passing with confidence, instead of failing with insecurity. Examination questions – together with answers – are furnished as the basic vehicle for study so that the mysteries of the examination and its compounding difficulties may be eliminated or diminished by a sure method.

This book is meant to help you pass your examination provided that you qualify and are serious in your objective.

The entire field is reviewed through the huge store of content information which is succinctly presented through a provocative and challenging approach – the question-and-answer method.

A climate of success is established by furnishing the correct answers at the end of each test.

You soon learn to recognize types of questions, forms of questions, and patterns of questioning. You may even begin to anticipate expected outcomes.

You perceive that many questions are repeated or adapted so that you can gain acute insights, which may enable you to score many sure points.

You learn how to confront new questions, or types of questions, and to attack them confidently and work out the correct answers.

You note objectives and emphases, and recognize pitfalls and dangers, so that you may make positive educational adjustments.

Moreover, you are kept fully informed in relation to new concepts, methods, practices, and directions in the field.

You discover that you arre actually taking the examination all the time: you are preparing for the examination by "taking" an examination, not by reading extraneous and/or supererogatory textbooks.

In short, this PASSBOOK®, used directedly, should be an important factor in helping you to pass your test.

SECRETARY II

DUTIES:

Under direction, performs a variety of secretarial duties and administrative tasks for one or more professional or management positions; interprets policies, administrative regulations, and the superior's viewpoint to others; may direct or coordinate the activities of a clerical support unit; performs related duties as required.

Performs tasks which fall into four broad categories: communication, coordination, organization and records maintenance. Within these categories, you would perform a variety of tasks which enable managers and program staff to accomplish the mission of the agency. You would review incoming correspondence and draft responses where appropriate; review outgoing correspondence; research background information; transmit instructions to staff and conduct follow-up. You would handle telephone calls and visitors and respond to questions; coordinate and arrange meetings; establish office procedures; design office filing systems; resolve day-to-day operational problems; coordinate information flow by acting as liaison among key executives, staff, other employees, and the public; and operate equipment which requires the manipulation of a standard alpha-numeric keyboard to produce correspondence, reports, and other agency documents. You would also supervise subordinate Secretary I's. Positions in this class are distinguished from Secretary I by the assignment of more administrative tasks, the scope and complexity of subject matter, and the requirement to exercise greater independence in acting for the superior.

SCOPE OF THE WRITTEN TEST:

The written test will be designed to test for knowledge, skills, and/or abilities in such areas as:

1. **Grammar/Usage/Punctuation** - The grammar and usage questions test for the ability to apply the basic rules of grammar and usage. The punctuation questions test for a knowledge of the correct placement of punctuation marks in sentences. You will be presented with sets of four sentences from each of which you must choose the sentence that contains a grammatical, usage, or punctuation error.

2. **Keyboarding practices** - These questions test for a knowledge of preferred practices in such areas as letter format, capitalization, hyphenation, plurals, possessives, word division, word and figure style for numbers, and common proofreading marks. In addition, there will be a passage to proofread followed by questions on how to correct the errors in the passage.

3. **Office practices** - These questions test for a knowledge of generally agreed-upon practices governing the handling of situations which typists, stenographers, secretaries, and office assistants encounter in their work, as well as a knowledge of efficient and effective methods used to accomplish office tasks. The questions cover such topics as planning work flow; setting priorities; dealing effectively with staff, visitors, and callers; filing and retrieving information; safeguarding confidentiality; using office equipment; and making procedural decisions and recommendations which contribute to a well-managed office.

4. **Office record keeping** - These questions test your ability to perform common office record keeping tasks. The test consists of two or more "sets" of questions, each set concerning a different problem. Typical record keeping problems might involve the organization or collation of data from several sources; scheduling; maintaining a record system using running balances; or completion of a table summarizing data using totals, subtotals, averages and percents.

5. **Spelling** - These questions test for the ability to spell words that are used in written business communications.

6. **Supervision** - These questions test for knowledge of the principles and practices employed in planning, organizing, and controlling the activities of a work unit toward predetermined objectives. The concepts covered, usually in a situational question format, include such topics as assigning and reviewing work; evaluating performance; maintaining work standards; motivating and developing subordinates; implementing procedural change; increasing efficiency; and dealing with problems of absenteeism, morale, and discipline.

HOW TO TAKE A TEST

I. YOU MUST PASS AN EXAMINATION

A. *WHAT EVERY CANDIDATE SHOULD KNOW*

Examination applicants often ask us for help in preparing for the written test. What can I study in advance? What kinds of questions will be asked? How will the test be given? How will the papers be graded?

As an applicant for a civil service examination, you may be wondering about some of these things. Our purpose here is to suggest effective methods of advance study and to describe civil service examinations.

Your chances for success on this examination can be increased if you know how to prepare. Those "pre-examination jitters" can be reduced if you know what to expect. You can even experience an adventure in good citizenship if you know why civil service exams are given.

B. *WHY ARE CIVIL SERVICE EXAMINATIONS GIVEN?*

Civil service examinations are important to you in two ways. As a citizen, you want public jobs filled by employees who know how to do their work. As a job seeker, you want a fair chance to compete for that job on an equal footing with other candidates. The best-known means of accomplishing this two-fold goal is the competitive examination.

Exams are widely publicized throughout the nation. They may be administered for jobs in federal, state, city, municipal, town or village governments or agencies.

Any citizen may apply, with some limitations, such as the age or residence of applicants. Your experience and education may be reviewed to see whether you meet the requirements for the particular examination. When these requirements exist, they are reasonable and applied consistently to all applicants. Thus, a competitive examination may cause you some uneasiness now, but it is your privilege and safeguard.

C. *HOW ARE CIVIL SERVICE EXAMS DEVELOPED?*

Examinations are carefully written by trained technicians who are specialists in the field known as "psychological measurement," in consultation with recognized authorities in the field of work that the test will cover. These experts recommend the subject matter areas or skills to be tested; only those knowledges or skills important to your success on the job are included. The most reliable books and source materials available are used as references. Together, the experts and technicians judge the difficulty level of the questions.

Test technicians know how to phrase questions so that the problem is clearly stated. Their ethics do not permit "trick" or "catch" questions. Questions may have been tried out on sample groups, or subjected to statistical analysis, to determine their usefulness.

Written tests are often used in combination with performance tests, ratings of training and experience, and oral interviews. All of these measures combine to form the best-known means of finding the right person for the right job.

II. HOW TO PASS THE WRITTEN TEST

A. *NATURE OF THE EXAMINATION*

To prepare intelligently for civil service examinations, you should know how they differ from school examinations you have taken. In school you were assigned certain definite pages to read or subjects to cover. The examination questions were quite detailed and usually emphasized memory. Civil service exams, on the other hand, try to discover your present ability to perform the duties of a position, plus your potentiality to learn these duties. In other words, a civil service exam attempts to predict how successful you will be. Questions cover such a broad area that they cannot be as minute and detailed as school exam questions.

In the public service similar kinds of work, or positions, are grouped together in one "class." This process is known as *position-classification*. All the positions in a class are paid according to the salary range for that class. One class title covers all of these positions, and they are all tested by the same examination.

B. *FOUR BASIC STEPS*

1) Study the announcement

How, then, can you know what subjects to study? Our best answer is: "Learn as much as possible about the class of positions for which you've applied." The exam will test the knowledge, skills and abilities needed to do the work.

Your most valuable source of information about the position you want is the official exam announcement. This announcement lists the training and experience qualifications. Check these standards and apply only if you come reasonably close to meeting them.

The brief description of the position in the examination announcement offers some clues to the subjects which will be tested. Think about the job itself. Review the duties in your mind. Can you perform them, or are there some in which you are rusty? Fill in the blank spots in your preparation.

Many jurisdictions preview the written test in the exam announcement by including a section called "Knowledge and Abilities Required," "Scope of the Examination," or some similar heading. Here you will find out specifically what fields will be tested.

2) Review your own background

Once you learn in general what the position is all about, and what you need to know to do the work, ask yourself which subjects you already know fairly well and which need improvement. You may wonder whether to concentrate on improving your strong areas or on building some background in your fields of weakness. When the announcement has specified "some knowledge" or "considerable knowledge," or has used adjectives like "beginning principles of..." or "advanced ... methods," you can get a clue as to the number and difficulty of questions to be asked in any given field. More questions, and hence broader coverage, would be included for those subjects which are more important in the work. Now weigh your strengths and weaknesses against the job requirements and prepare accordingly.

3) Determine the level of the position

Another way to tell how intensively you should prepare is to understand the level of the job for which you are applying. Is it the entering level? In other words, is this the position in which beginners in a field of work are hired? Or is it an intermediate or advanced level? Sometimes this is indicated by such words as "Junior" or "Senior" in the class title. Other jurisdictions use Roman numerals to designate the level – Clerk I, Clerk II, for example. The word "Supervisor" sometimes appears in the title. If the level is not indicated by the title, check the description of duties. Will you be working under very close supervision, or will you have responsibility for independent decisions in this work?

4) Choose appropriate study materials

Now that you know the subjects to be examined and the relative amount of each subject to be covered, you can choose suitable study materials. For beginning level jobs, or even advanced ones, if you have a pronounced weakness in some aspect of your training, read a modern, standard textbook in that field. Be sure it is up to date and has general coverage. Such books are normally available at your library, and the librarian will be glad to help you locate one. For entry-level positions, questions of appropriate difficulty are chosen – neither highly advanced questions, nor those too simple. Such questions require careful thought but not advanced training.

If the position for which you are applying is technical or advanced, you will read more advanced, specialized material. If you are already familiar with the basic principles of your field, elementary textbooks would waste your time. Concentrate on advanced textbooks and technical periodicals. Think through the concepts and review difficult problems in your field.

These are all general sources. You can get more ideas on your own initiative, following these leads. For example, training manuals and publications of the government agency which employs workers in your field can be useful, particularly for technical and professional positions. A letter or visit to the government department involved may result in more specific study suggestions, and certainly will provide you with a more definite idea of the exact nature of the position you are seeking.

III. KINDS OF TESTS

Tests are used for purposes other than measuring knowledge and ability to perform specified duties. For some positions, it is equally important to test ability to make adjustments to new situations or to profit from training. In others, basic mental abilities not dependent on information are essential. Questions which test these things may not appear as pertinent to the duties of the position as those which test for knowledge and information. Yet they are often highly important parts of a fair examination. For very general questions, it is almost impossible to help you direct your study efforts. What we can do is to point out some of the more common of these general abilities needed in public service positions and describe some typical questions.

1) General information

Broad, general information has been found useful for predicting job success in some kinds of work. This is tested in a variety of ways, from vocabulary lists to questions about current events. Basic background in some field of work, such as sociology or economics, may be sampled in a group of questions. Often these are principles which have become familiar to most persons through exposure rather than through formal training. It is difficult to advise you how to study for these questions; being alert to the world around you is our best suggestion.

2) Verbal ability

An example of an ability needed in many positions is verbal or language ability. Verbal ability is, in brief, the ability to use and understand words. Vocabulary and grammar tests are typical measures of this ability. Reading comprehension or paragraph interpretation questions are common in many kinds of civil service tests. You are given a paragraph of written material and asked to find its central meaning.

3) Numerical ability

Number skills can be tested by the familiar arithmetic problem, by checking paired lists of numbers to see which are alike and which are different, or by interpreting charts and graphs. In the latter test, a graph may be printed in the test booklet which you are asked to use as the basis for answering questions.

4) Observation

A popular test for law-enforcement positions is the observation test. A picture is shown to you for several minutes, then taken away. Questions about the picture test your ability to observe both details and larger elements.

5) Following directions

In many positions in the public service, the employee must be able to carry out written instructions dependably and accurately. You may be given a chart with several columns, each column listing a variety of information. The questions require you to carry out directions involving the information given in the chart.

6) Skills and aptitudes

Performance tests effectively measure some manual skills and aptitudes. When the skill is one in which you are trained, such as typing or shorthand, you can practice. These tests are often very much like those given in business school or high school courses. For many of the other skills and aptitudes, however, no short-time preparation can be made. Skills and abilities natural to you or that you have developed throughout your lifetime are being tested.

Many of the general questions just described provide all the data needed to answer the questions and ask you to use your reasoning ability to find the answers. Your best preparation for these tests, as well as for tests of facts and ideas, is to be at your physical and mental best. You, no doubt, have your own methods of getting into an exam-taking mood and keeping "in shape." The next section lists some ideas on this subject.

IV. KINDS OF QUESTIONS

Only rarely is the "essay" question, which you answer in narrative form, used in civil service tests. Civil service tests are usually of the short-answer type. Full instructions for answering these questions will be given to you at the examination. But in case this is your first experience with short-answer questions and separate answer sheets, here is what you need to know:

1) Multiple-choice Questions

Most popular of the short-answer questions is the "multiple choice" or "best answer" question. It can be used, for example, to test for factual knowledge, ability to solve problems or judgment in meeting situations found at work.

A multiple-choice question is normally one of three types—

- It can begin with an incomplete statement followed by several possible endings. You are to find the one ending which *best* completes the statement, although some of the others may not be entirely wrong.
- It can also be a complete statement in the form of a question which is answered by choosing one of the statements listed.
- It can be in the form of a problem – again you select the best answer.

Here is an example of a multiple-choice question with a discussion which should give you some clues as to the method for choosing the right answer:

When an employee has a complaint about his assignment, the action which will *best* help him overcome his difficulty is to
- A. discuss his difficulty with his coworkers
- B. take the problem to the head of the organization
- C. take the problem to the person who gave him the assignment
- D. say nothing to anyone about his complaint

In answering this question, you should study each of the choices to find which is best. Consider choice "A" – Certainly an employee may discuss his complaint with fellow employees, but no change or improvement can result, and the complaint remains unresolved. Choice "B" is a poor choice since the head of the organization probably does not know what assignment you have been given, and taking your problem to him is known as "going over the head" of the supervisor. The supervisor, or person who made the assignment, is the person who can clarify it or correct any injustice. Choice "C" is, therefore, correct. To say nothing, as in choice "D," is unwise. Supervisors have and interest in knowing the problems employees are facing, and the employee is seeking a solution to his problem.

2) True/False Questions

The "true/false" or "right/wrong" form of question is sometimes used. Here a complete statement is given. Your job is to decide whether the statement is right or wrong.

SAMPLE: A roaming cell-phone call to a nearby city costs less than a non-roaming call to a distant city.

This statement is wrong, or false, since roaming calls are more expensive.

This is not a complete list of all possible question forms, although most of the others are variations of these common types. You will always get complete directions for answering questions. Be sure you understand *how* to mark your answers – ask questions until you do.

V. RECORDING YOUR ANSWERS

Computer terminals are used more and more today for many different kinds of exams.

For an examination with very few applicants, you may be told to record your answers in the test booklet itself. Separate answer sheets are much more common. If this separate answer sheet is to be scored by machine – and this is often the case – it is highly important that you mark your answers correctly in order to get credit.

An electronic scoring machine is often used in civil service offices because of the speed with which papers can be scored. Machine-scored answer sheets must be marked with a pencil, which will be given to you. This pencil has a high graphite content which responds to the electronic scoring machine. As a matter of fact, stray dots may register as answers, so do not let your pencil rest on the answer sheet while you are pondering the correct answer. Also, if your pencil lead breaks or is otherwise defective, ask for another.

Since the answer sheet will be dropped in a slot in the scoring machine, be careful not to bend the corners or get the paper crumpled.

The answer sheet normally has five vertical columns of numbers, with 30 numbers to a column. These numbers correspond to the question numbers in your test booklet. After each number, going across the page are four or five pairs of dotted lines. These short dotted lines have small letters or numbers above them. The first two pairs may also have a "T" or "F" above the letters. This indicates that the first two pairs only are to be used if the questions are of the true-false type. If the questions are multiple choice, disregard the "T" and "F" and pay attention only to the small letters or numbers.

Answer your questions in the manner of the sample that follows:

32. The largest city in the United States is
    A. Washington, D.C.
    B. New York City
    C. Chicago
    D. Detroit
    E. San Francisco

1) Choose the answer you think is best. (New York City is the largest, so "B" is correct.)
2) Find the row of dotted lines numbered the same as the question you are answering. (Find row number 32)
3) Find the pair of dotted lines corresponding to the answer. (Find the pair of lines under the mark "B.")
4) Make a solid black mark between the dotted lines.

VI. BEFORE THE TEST

Common sense will help you find procedures to follow to get ready for an examination. Too many of us, however, overlook these sensible measures. Indeed, nervousness and fatigue have been found to be the most serious reasons why applicants fail to do their best on civil service tests. Here is a list of reminders:

- Begin your preparation early – Don't wait until the last minute to go scurrying around for books and materials or to find out what the position is all about.
- Prepare continuously – An hour a night for a week is better than an all-night cram session. This has been definitely established. What is more, a night a week for a month will return better dividends than crowding your study into a shorter period of time.
- Locate the place of the exam – You have been sent a notice telling you when and where to report for the examination. If the location is in a different town or otherwise unfamiliar to you, it would be well to inquire the best route and learn something about the building.
- Relax the night before the test – Allow your mind to rest. Do not study at all that night. Plan some mild recreation or diversion; then go to bed early and get a good night's sleep.
- Get up early enough to make a leisurely trip to the place for the test – This way unforeseen events, traffic snarls, unfamiliar buildings, etc. will not upset you.
- Dress comfortably – A written test is not a fashion show. You will be known by number and not by name, so wear something comfortable.
- Leave excess paraphernalia at home – Shopping bags and odd bundles will get in your way. You need bring only the items mentioned in the official notice you received; usually everything you need is provided. Do not bring reference books to the exam. They will only confuse those last minutes and be taken away from you when in the test room.
- Arrive somewhat ahead of time – If because of transportation schedules you must get there very early, bring a newspaper or magazine to take your mind off yourself while waiting.
- Locate the examination room – When you have found the proper room, you will be directed to the seat or part of the room where you will sit. Sometimes you are given a sheet of instructions to read while you are waiting. Do not fill out any forms until you are told to do so; just read them and be prepared.
- Relax and prepare to listen to the instructions
- If you have any physical problem that may keep you from doing your best, be sure to tell the test administrator. If you are sick or in poor health, you really cannot do your best on the exam. You can come back and take the test some other time.

VII. AT THE TEST

The day of the test is here and you have the test booklet in your hand. The temptation to get going is very strong. Caution! There is more to success than knowing the right answers. You must know how to identify your papers and understand variations in the type of short-answer question used in this particular examination. Follow these suggestions for maximum results from your efforts:

1) Cooperate with the monitor

The test administrator has a duty to create a situation in which you can be as much at ease as possible. He will give instructions, tell you when to begin, check to see that you are marking your answer sheet correctly, and so on. He is not there to guard you, although he will see that your competitors do not take unfair advantage. He wants to help you do your best.

2) Listen to all instructions

Don't jump the gun! Wait until you understand all directions. In most civil service tests you get more time than you need to answer the questions. So don't be in a hurry. Read each word of instructions until you clearly understand the meaning. Study the examples, listen to all announcements and follow directions. Ask questions if you do not understand what to do.

3) Identify your papers

Civil service exams are usually identified by number only. You will be assigned a number; you must not put your name on your test papers. Be sure to copy your number correctly. Since more than one exam may be given, copy your exact examination title.

4) Plan your time

Unless you are told that a test is a "speed" or "rate of work" test, speed itself is usually not important. Time enough to answer all the questions will be provided, but this does not mean that you have all day. An overall time limit has been set. Divide the total time (in minutes) by the number of questions to determine the approximate time you have for each question.

5) Do not linger over difficult questions

If you come across a difficult question, mark it with a paper clip (useful to have along) and come back to it when you have been through the booklet. One caution if you do this – be sure to skip a number on your answer sheet as well. Check often to be sure that you have not lost your place and that you are marking in the row numbered the same as the question you are answering.

6) Read the questions

Be sure you know what the question asks! Many capable people are unsuccessful because they failed to *read* the questions correctly.

7) Answer all questions

Unless you have been instructed that a penalty will be deducted for incorrect answers, it is better to guess than to omit a question.

8) Speed tests

It is often better NOT to guess on speed tests. It has been found that on timed tests people are tempted to spend the last few seconds before time is called in marking answers at random – without even reading them – in the hope of picking up a few extra points. To discourage this practice, the instructions may warn you that your score will be "corrected" for guessing. That is, a penalty will be applied. The incorrect answers will be deducted from the correct ones, or some other penalty formula will be used.

9) Review your answers

If you finish before time is called, go back to the questions you guessed or omitted to give them further thought. Review other answers if you have time.

10) Return your test materials

If you are ready to leave before others have finished or time is called, take ALL your materials to the monitor and leave quietly. Never take any test material with you. The monitor can discover whose papers are not complete, and taking a test booklet may be grounds for disqualification.

VIII. EXAMINATION TECHNIQUES

1) Read the general instructions carefully. These are usually printed on the first page of the exam booklet. As a rule, these instructions refer to the timing of the examination; the fact that you should not start work until the signal and must stop work at a signal, etc. If there are any *special* instructions, such as a choice of questions to be answered, make sure that you note this instruction carefully.

2) When you are ready to start work on the examination, that is as soon as the signal has been given, read the instructions to each question booklet, underline any key words or phrases, such as *least*, *best*, *outline*, *describe* and the like. In this way you will tend to answer as requested rather than discover on reviewing your paper that you *listed without describing*, that you selected the *worst* choice rather than the *best* choice, etc.

3) If the examination is of the objective or multiple-choice type – that is, each question will also give a series of possible answers: A, B, C or D, and you are called upon to select the best answer and write the letter next to that answer on your answer paper – it is advisable to start answering each question in turn. There may be anywhere from 50 to 100 such questions in the three or four hours allotted and you can see how much time would be taken if you read through all the questions before beginning to answer any. Furthermore, if you come across a question or group of questions which you know would be difficult to answer, it would undoubtedly affect your handling of all the other questions.

4) If the examination is of the essay type and contains but a few questions, it is a moot point as to whether you should read all the questions before starting to answer any one. Of course, if you are given a choice – say five out of seven and the like – then it is essential to read all the questions so you can eliminate the two that are most difficult. If, however, you are asked to answer all the questions, there may be danger in trying to answer the easiest one first because you may find that you will spend too much time on it. The best technique is to answer the first question, then proceed to the second, etc.

5) Time your answers. Before the exam begins, write down the time it started, then add the time allowed for the examination and write down the time it must be completed, then divide the time available somewhat as follows:

- If 3-1/2 hours are allowed, that would be 210 minutes. If you have 80 objective-type questions, that would be an average of 2-1/2 minutes per question. Allow yourself no more than 2 minutes per question, or a total of 160 minutes, which will permit about 50 minutes to review.
- If for the time allotment of 210 minutes there are 7 essay questions to answer, that would average about 30 minutes a question. Give yourself only 25 minutes per question so that you have about 35 minutes to review.

6) The most important instruction is to *read each question* and make sure you know what is wanted. The second most important instruction is to *time yourself properly* so that you answer every question. The third most important instruction is to *answer every question*. Guess if you have to but include something for each question. Remember that you will receive no credit for a blank and will probably receive some credit if you write something in answer to an essay question. If you guess a letter – say "B" for a multiple-choice question – you may have guessed right. If you leave a blank as an answer to a multiple-choice question, the examiners may respect your feelings but it will not add a point to your score. Some exams may penalize you for wrong answers, so in such cases *only*, you may not want to guess unless you have some basis for your answer.

7) Suggestions
   a. Objective-type questions
      1. Examine the question booklet for proper sequence of pages and questions
      2. Read all instructions carefully
      3. Skip any question which seems too difficult; return to it after all other questions have been answered
      4. Apportion your time properly; do not spend too much time on any single question or group of questions
      5. Note and underline key words – *all, most, fewest, least, best, worst, same, opposite,* etc.
      6. Pay particular attention to negatives
      7. Note unusual option, e.g., unduly long, short, complex, different or similar in content to the body of the question
      8. Observe the use of "hedging" words – *probably, may, most likely,* etc.
      9. Make sure that your answer is put next to the same number as the question
      10. Do not second-guess unless you have good reason to believe the second answer is definitely more correct
      11. Cross out original answer if you decide another answer is more accurate; do not erase until you are ready to hand your paper in
      12. Answer all questions; guess unless instructed otherwise
      13. Leave time for review

   b. Essay questions
      1. Read each question carefully
      2. Determine exactly what is wanted. Underline key words or phrases.
      3. Decide on outline or paragraph answer

4. Include many different points and elements unless asked to develop any one or two points or elements
5. Show impartiality by giving pros and cons unless directed to select one side only
6. Make and write down any assumptions you find necessary to answer the questions
7. Watch your English, grammar, punctuation and choice of words
8. Time your answers; don't crowd material

8) Answering the essay question

Most essay questions can be answered by framing the specific response around several key words or ideas. Here are a few such key words or ideas:

M's: manpower, materials, methods, money, management
P's: purpose, program, policy, plan, procedure, practice, problems, pitfalls, personnel, public relations
   a. Six basic steps in handling problems:
      1. Preliminary plan and background development
      2. Collect information, data and facts
      3. Analyze and interpret information, data and facts
      4. Analyze and develop solutions as well as make recommendations
      5. Prepare report and sell recommendations
      6. Install recommendations and follow up effectiveness

   b. Pitfalls to avoid
      1. *Taking things for granted* – A statement of the situation does not necessarily imply that each of the elements is necessarily true; for example, a complaint may be invalid and biased so that all that can be taken for granted is that a complaint has been registered
      2. *Considering only one side of a situation* – Wherever possible, indicate several alternatives and then point out the reasons you selected the best one
      3. *Failing to indicate follow up* – Whenever your answer indicates action on your part, make certain that you will take proper follow-up action to see how successful your recommendations, procedures or actions turn out to be
      4. *Taking too long in answering any single question* – Remember to time your answers properly

IX. AFTER THE TEST

Scoring procedures differ in detail among civil service jurisdictions although the general principles are the same. Whether the papers are hand-scored or graded by machine we have described, they are nearly always graded by number. That is, the person who marks the paper knows only the number – never the name – of the applicant. Not until all the papers have been graded will they be matched with names. If other tests, such as training and experience or oral interview ratings have been given, scores will be combined. Different parts of the examination usually have different weights. For example, the written test might count 60 percent of the final grade, and a rating of training and experience 40 percent. In many jurisdictions, veterans will have a certain number of points added to their grades.

After the final grade has been determined, the names are placed in grade order and an eligible list is established. There are various methods for resolving ties between those who get the same final grade – probably the most common is to place first the name of the person whose application was received first. Job offers are made from the eligible list in the order the names appear on it. You will be notified of your grade and your rank as soon as all these computations have been made. This will be done as rapidly as possible.

People who are found to meet the requirements in the announcement are called "eligibles." Their names are put on a list of eligible candidates. An eligible's chances of getting a job depend on how high he stands on this list and how fast agencies are filling jobs from the list.

When a job is to be filled from a list of eligibles, the agency asks for the names of people on the list of eligibles for that job. When the civil service commission receives this request, it sends to the agency the names of the three people highest on this list. Or, if the job to be filled has specialized requirements, the office sends the agency the names of the top three persons who meet these requirements from the general list.

The appointing officer makes a choice from among the three people whose names were sent to him. If the selected person accepts the appointment, the names of the others are put back on the list to be considered for future openings.

That is the rule in hiring from all kinds of eligible lists, whether they are for typist, carpenter, chemist, or something else. For every vacancy, the appointing officer has his choice of any one of the top three eligibles on the list. This explains why the person whose name is on top of the list sometimes does not get an appointment when some of the persons lower on the list do. If the appointing officer chooses the second or third eligible, the No. 1 eligible does not get a job at once, but stays on the list until he is appointed or the list is terminated.

X. HOW TO PASS THE INTERVIEW TEST

The examination for which you applied requires an oral interview test. You have already taken the written test and you are now being called for the interview test – the final part of the formal examination.

You may think that it is not possible to prepare for an interview test and that there are no procedures to follow during an interview. Our purpose is to point out some things you can do in advance that will help you and some good rules to follow and pitfalls to avoid while you are being interviewed.

What is an interview supposed to test?
The written examination is designed to test the technical knowledge and competence of the candidate; the oral is designed to evaluate intangible qualities, not readily measured otherwise, and to establish a list showing the relative fitness of each candidate – as measured against his competitors – for the position sought. Scoring is not on the basis of "right" and "wrong," but on a sliding scale of values ranging from "not passable" to "outstanding." As a matter of fact, it is possible to achieve a relatively low score without a single "incorrect" answer because of evident weakness in the qualities being measured.

Occasionally, an examination may consist entirely of an oral test – either an individual or a group oral. In such cases, information is sought concerning the technical knowledges and abilities of the candidate, since there has been no written examination for this purpose. More commonly, however, an oral test is used to supplement a written examination.

Who conducts interviews?

The composition of oral boards varies among different jurisdictions. In nearly all, a representative of the personnel department serves as chairman. One of the members of the board may be a representative of the department in which the candidate would work. In some cases, "outside experts" are used, and, frequently, a businessman or some other representative of the general public is asked to serve. Labor and management or other special groups may be represented. The aim is to secure the services of experts in the appropriate field.

However the board is composed, it is a good idea (and not at all improper or unethical) to ascertain in advance of the interview who the members are and what groups they represent. When you are introduced to them, you will have some idea of their backgrounds and interests, and at least you will not stutter and stammer over their names.

What should be done before the interview?

While knowledge about the board members is useful and takes some of the surprise element out of the interview, there is other preparation which is more substantive. It *is* possible to prepare for an oral interview – in several ways:

1) Keep a copy of your application and review it carefully before the interview

This may be the only document before the oral board, and the starting point of the interview. Know what education and experience you have listed there, and the sequence and dates of all of it. Sometimes the board will ask you to review the highlights of your experience for them; you should not have to hem and haw doing it.

2) Study the class specification and the examination announcement

Usually, the oral board has one or both of these to guide them. The qualities, characteristics or knowledges required by the position sought are stated in these documents. They offer valuable clues as to the nature of the oral interview. For example, if the job involves supervisory responsibilities, the announcement will usually indicate that knowledge of modern supervisory methods and the qualifications of the candidate as a supervisor will be tested. If so, you can expect such questions, frequently in the form of a hypothetical situation which you are expected to solve. NEVER go into an oral without knowledge of the duties and responsibilities of the job you seek.

3) Think through each qualification required

Try to visualize the kind of questions you would ask if you were a board member. How well could you answer them? Try especially to appraise your own knowledge and background in each area, *measured against the job sought*, and identify any areas in which you are weak. Be critical and realistic – do not flatter yourself.

4) Do some general reading in areas in which you feel you may be weak

For example, if the job involves supervision and your past experience has NOT, some general reading in supervisory methods and practices, particularly in the field of human relations, might be useful. Do NOT study agency procedures or detailed manuals. The oral board will be testing your understanding and capacity, not your memory.

5) Get a good night's sleep and watch your general health and mental attitude

You will want a clear head at the interview. Take care of a cold or any other minor ailment, and of course, no hangovers.

What should be done on the day of the interview?

Now comes the day of the interview itself. Give yourself plenty of time to get there. Plan to arrive somewhat ahead of the scheduled time, particularly if your appointment is in the fore part of the day. If a previous candidate fails to appear, the board might be ready for you a bit early. By early afternoon an oral board is almost invariably behind schedule if there are many candidates, and you may have to wait. Take along a book or magazine to read, or your application to review, but leave any extraneous material in the waiting room when you go in for your interview. In any event, relax and compose yourself.

The matter of dress is important. The board is forming impressions about you – from your experience, your manners, your attitude, and your appearance. Give your personal appearance careful attention. Dress your best, but not your flashiest. Choose conservative, appropriate clothing, and be sure it is immaculate. This is a business interview, and your appearance should indicate that you regard it as such. Besides, being well groomed and properly dressed will help boost your confidence.

Sooner or later, someone will call your name and escort you into the interview room. *This is it.* From here on you are on your own. It is too late for any more preparation. But remember, you asked for this opportunity to prove your fitness, and you are here because your request was granted.

What happens when you go in?

The usual sequence of events will be as follows: The clerk (who is often the board stenographer) will introduce you to the chairman of the oral board, who will introduce you to the other members of the board. Acknowledge the introductions before you sit down. Do not be surprised if you find a microphone facing you or a stenotypist sitting by. Oral interviews are usually recorded in the event of an appeal or other review.

Usually the chairman of the board will open the interview by reviewing the highlights of your education and work experience from your application – primarily for the benefit of the other members of the board, as well as to get the material into the record. Do not interrupt or comment unless there is an error or significant misinterpretation; if that is the case, do not hesitate. But do not quibble about insignificant matters. Also, he will usually ask you some question about your education, experience or your present job – partly to get you to start talking and to establish the interviewing "rapport." He may start the actual questioning, or turn it over to one of the other members. Frequently, each member undertakes the questioning on a particular area, one in which he is perhaps most competent, so you can expect each member to participate in the examination. Because time is limited, you may also expect some rather abrupt switches in the direction the questioning takes, so do not be upset by it. Normally, a board member will not pursue a single line of questioning unless he discovers a particular strength or weakness.

After each member has participated, the chairman will usually ask whether any member has any further questions, then will ask you if you have anything you wish to add. Unless you are expecting this question, it may floor you. Worse, it may start you off on an extended, extemporaneous speech. The board is not usually seeking more information. The question is principally to offer you a last opportunity to present further qualifications or to indicate that you have nothing to add. So, if you feel that a significant qualification or characteristic has been overlooked, it is proper to point it out in a sentence or so. Do not compliment the board on the thoroughness of their examination – they have been sketchy, and you know it. If you wish, merely say, "No thank you, I have nothing further to add." This is a point where you can "talk yourself out" of a good impression or fail to present an important bit of information. Remember, *you close the interview yourself.*

The chairman will then say, "That is all, Mr. _____, thank you." Do not be startled; the interview is over, and quicker than you think. Thank him, gather your belongings and take your leave. Save your sigh of relief for the other side of the door.

How to put your best foot forward

Throughout this entire process, you may feel that the board individually and collectively is trying to pierce your defenses, seek out your hidden weaknesses and embarrass and confuse you. Actually, this is not true. They are obliged to make an appraisal of your qualifications for the job you are seeking, and they want to see you in your best light. Remember, they must interview all candidates and a non-cooperative candidate may become a failure in spite of their best efforts to bring out his qualifications. Here are 15 suggestions that will help you:

1) Be natural – Keep your attitude confident, not cocky

If you are not confident that you can do the job, do not expect the board to be. Do not apologize for your weaknesses, try to bring out your strong points. The board is interested in a positive, not negative, presentation. Cockiness will antagonize any board member and make him wonder if you are covering up a weakness by a false show of strength.

2) Get comfortable, but don't lounge or sprawl

Sit erectly but not stiffly. A careless posture may lead the board to conclude that you are careless in other things, or at least that you are not impressed by the importance of the occasion. Either conclusion is natural, even if incorrect. Do not fuss with your clothing, a pencil or an ashtray. Your hands may occasionally be useful to emphasize a point; do not let them become a point of distraction.

3) Do not wisecrack or make small talk

This is a serious situation, and your attitude should show that you consider it as such. Further, the time of the board is limited – they do not want to waste it, and neither should you.

4) Do not exaggerate your experience or abilities

In the first place, from information in the application or other interviews and sources, the board may know more about you than you think. Secondly, you probably will not get away with it. An experienced board is rather adept at spotting such a situation, so do not take the chance.

5) If you know a board member, do not make a point of it, yet do not hide it

Certainly you are not fooling him, and probably not the other members of the board. Do not try to take advantage of your acquaintanceship – it will probably do you little good.

6) Do not dominate the interview

Let the board do that. They will give you the clues – do not assume that you have to do all the talking. Realize that the board has a number of questions to ask you, and do not try to take up all the interview time by showing off your extensive knowledge of the answer to the first one.

7) Be attentive

You only have 20 minutes or so, and you should keep your attention at its sharpest throughout. When a member is addressing a problem or question to you, give him your undivided attention. Address your reply principally to him, but do not exclude the other board members.

8) Do not interrupt

A board member may be stating a problem for you to analyze. He will ask you a question when the time comes. Let him state the problem, and wait for the question.

9) Make sure you understand the question

Do not try to answer until you are sure what the question is. If it is not clear, restate it in your own words or ask the board member to clarify it for you. However, do not haggle about minor elements.

10) Reply promptly but not hastily

A common entry on oral board rating sheets is "candidate responded readily," or "candidate hesitated in replies." Respond as promptly and quickly as you can, but do not jump to a hasty, ill-considered answer.

11) Do not be peremptory in your answers

A brief answer is proper – but do not fire your answer back. That is a losing game from your point of view. The board member can probably ask questions much faster than you can answer them.

12) Do not try to create the answer you think the board member wants

He is interested in what kind of mind you have and how it works – not in playing games. Furthermore, he can usually spot this practice and will actually grade you down on it.

13) Do not switch sides in your reply merely to agree with a board member

Frequently, a member will take a contrary position merely to draw you out and to see if you are willing and able to defend your point of view. Do not start a debate, yet do not surrender a good position. If a position is worth taking, it is worth defending.

14) Do not be afraid to admit an error in judgment if you are shown to be wrong

The board knows that you are forced to reply without any opportunity for careful consideration. Your answer may be demonstrably wrong. If so, admit it and get on with the interview.

15) Do not dwell at length on your present job

The opening question may relate to your present assignment. Answer the question but do not go into an extended discussion. You are being examined for a *new* job, not your present one. As a matter of fact, try to phrase ALL your answers in terms of the job for which you are being examined.

Basis of Rating

Probably you will forget most of these "do's" and "don'ts" when you walk into the oral interview room. Even remembering them all will not ensure you a passing grade. Perhaps you did not have the qualifications in the first place. But remembering them will help you to put your best foot forward, without treading on the toes of the board members.

Rumor and popular opinion to the contrary notwithstanding, an oral board wants you to make the best appearance possible. They know you are under pressure – but they also want to see how you respond to it as a guide to what your reaction would be under the pressures of the job you seek. They will be influenced by the degree of poise you display, the personal traits you show and the manner in which you respond.

ABOUT THIS BOOK

This book contains tests divided into Examination Sections. Go through each test, answering every question in the margin. At the end of each test look at the answer key and check your answers. On the ones you got wrong, look at the right answer choice and learn. Do not fill in the answers first. Do not memorize the questions and answers, but understand the answer and principles involved. On your test, the questions will likely be different from the samples. Questions are changed and new ones added. If you understand these past questions you should have success with any changes that arise. Tests may consist of several types of questions. We have additional books on each subject should more study be advisable or necessary for you. Finally, the more you study, the better prepared you will be. This book is intended to be the last thing you study before you walk into the examination room. Prior study of relevant texts is also recommended. NLC publishes some of these in our Fundamental Series. Knowledge and good sense are important factors in passing your exam. Good luck also helps. So now study this Passbook, absorb the material contained within and take that knowledge into the examination. Then do your best to pass that exam.

———

EXAMINATION SECTION

EXAMINATION SECTION

TEST 1

DIRECTIONS: Each question or incomplete statement is followed by several suggested answers or completions. Select the one that *BEST* answers the question or completes the statement. *PRINT THE LETTER OF THE CORRECT ANSWER IN THE SPACE AT THE RIGHT.*

1. Employees tend to band together in small informal groups. Considering the effective processing of the work loads these groups *GENERALLY* should be
   A. ignored since they have no relation at all to the formal organization
   B. strongly discouraged since they result in much time wasted on personal conversations
   C. tolerated since they provide needed diversion from work pressure
   D. disbanded since they disrupt office activities

1._____

2. It is *GENERALLY* agreed that the soundest of the following approaches to speeding up the flow of work in an office is to
   A. reduce the clerical staff by a small percentage
   B. develop a work simplification program in which employees participate in improving work methods
   C. retain major office machines beyond the suggested replacement dates
   D. have employees keep accounts of all supplies used

2._____

3. Of the following, the one which usually *BEST* encourages group cohesiveness is
   A. setting up an opportunity for competition among the members
   B. creating opportunities for group members to communicate with each other
   C. increasing the size of the group
   D. pointing out to the group the most effective members of the group in each office

3._____

4. Suppose that a student arrives for an appointment with a professor while you, the professor's secretary, are typing an important memo. Of the following, it would normally be *BEST* for you to
   A. explain that you have a very important memo to type and request that the student have a seat
   B. finish typing the memo before acknowledging the student's presence
   C. point out the professor's office and tell the student to go right in
   D. stop typing, check to be sure the professor is free, and then escort the student into the professor's office

4._____

5. Upward communications in an organization are MOST generally facilitated when
   A. messages are carefully screened by the first-line supervisors
   B. there is a clear line of movement of messages upward so that messages flow quickly and everyone understands the movement
   C. there is a lack of acceptance of criticism from subordinates
   D. the types of messages that are acceptable are specified exactly

5._____

6. Suppose that a student enters your office and asks to see a Professor Carison. 6._____
   The student is in the wrong office and you do not know where Professor Carlson
   is located. Of the following, it would *generally* be *BEST* for you to
   A. ask the student to wait while you check the office directory
   B. direct the student to an information desk on another floor
   C. politely inform the student that you do not know where Professor Carlson is
      located and therefore cannot offer assistance
   D. suggest that the student try the office next door

7. Suppose that another office assistant tells you: "I would never take anything of great 7._____
   value from the office, but who is going to miss a few pencils and scotch tape? I take
   these things regularly." Of the following, the *BEST* way for you to react to this
   statement *generally* should be to
   A. agree with the office assistant and tell her that these small items don't add up to
      much in the huge budget of the college
   B. comment to the office assistant that she shouldn't worry at all about taking items
      because others are doing the same thing and it is just accepted
   C. comment to the office assistant that the principle of honesty applies irrespective
      of the dollar value of the items taken
   D. refrain from making any comment since nothing would be gained by further
      discussion on such a topic

8. A certain office assistant has a poor tardiness record and was recently warned by her 8._____
   supervisor that certain disciplinary action would be taken if she were late again.
   If she comes in late again, in private, the supervisor *SHOULD*
   A. speak to her right away and, after listening to her explanation, impose any
      warranted discipline quietly and impersonally
   B. speak to her during the next afternoon this will prevent an emotional
      confrontation and will give her time to fully realize the consequences of her
      actions
   C. speak to her right away and make an attempt to soften the necessary disciplinary
      action by apologizing for having to use discipline
   D. speak to her right away, and remind her in no uncertain terms of the difficulty she
      has caused him by her continual lateness before imposing any warranted
      discipline

9. Suppose that you are a secretary to a professor who has been called to an 9._____
   emergency conference fifteen minutes before a scheduled appointment with a
   student. When the student arrives, you normally should apologize for the
   inconvenience *and,* if no appointment with him is available the same day,
   A. arrange for another professor to see the student if the matter is one which can be
      handled by someone else
   B. make a tentative appointment for a later date even if you do not know the
      professor's schedule
   C. request that the student call for another appointment
   D. request that the student wait even if it is unknown how long the professor will be
      away

10. Of the following, it is *generally* agreed that the *BEST* way to get feedback as to   10._____
whether information communicated has been understood is to ask the person who
has received the information
    A. whether information just communicated was understood
    B. whether there are any questions about the information just communicated
    C. questions about the information that require yes or no answers
    D. questions that require use of the information in answering

11. One aspect of stereotyping and evaluating the source is the tendency to ignore the   11._____
"grays" and to react in "black or white" terms. Thus, when someone is speaking who
has gained our trust or who begins a speech by saying something with which we
agree, we will hear nearly everything he says as good and correct. On the other
hand, someone we distrust will be ignored or heard to say nothing worth attending
to.

    This failure to discriminate between the "good" and "bad" that may be intermixed
    within a single person and his comments is *MOST* appropriately referred to as
    A. the negative feedback   B. bureaucracy
    C. the halo effect   D. Parkinson's law

12. A supervisory approach in which each phase of the job is specified in detail,   12._____
supervision is close, and people are allowed little discretion in performing their jobs,
MOST GENERALLY
    A. is preferred by most subordinates and provides motivation to work harder
    B. provides little or no incentive to work harder than the minimum required
    C. creates undue pressure which usually results in increased performance
    D. works better in the long run than in the short run

13. Those who have studied the phenomenon of the office "grapevine" *MOST*   13._____
GENERALLY have found that
    A. the truth is always conveyed via the "grapevine"
    B. the "grapevine" often performs a useful service by correcting some of the
        shortcomings of the formal communication system
    C. the "grapevine" naturally interferes with the satisfactory functioning of the formal
        communication system which has been established
    D. efforts to destroy the "grapevine" are successful

14. It is *generally* agreed that on-the-job training is *MOST* effective when new   14._____
employees are
    A. allowed to watch highly skilled employees perform the job and subsequently
        follow the same procedures on their own
    B. shown the job operations step by step and allowed to practice under close
        supervision
    C. provided with procedures manuals that outline the job operations in clear,
        easy-to-understand language, instead of receiving personal instructions
    D. put to work immediately for motivational purposes and then learn job routines
        principally by trial and error

15. The supervisor criticizes an office assistant who, although a good worker, is consistently late in the morning, although she lives just a short subway ride away from the office. She is also late after lunch. The *MOST* desirable reaction for the office assistant in such a situation is to
    A. realize that many of her friends are also late but they have nicer supervisors so there is really no need to note what the supervisor said to her
    B. keep track of others who are late and remind the supervisor that others are also late
    C. realize that she should be prompt and make adjustments in her activities so that in the future she does get to work on time
    D. realize that she is one of the better workers and is able to accomplish as much in an hour as the average worker accomplishes in two hours
15._____

16. When a supervisor finds it necessary to let a subordinate know that he is dissatisfied with the subordinate's level of performance, which of the following tactics would usually prove *MOST* effective in improving the subordinate's performance?
    A. The supervisor should be angry when criticizing in order to prevent the mistakes from recurring.
    B. Once criticism has been made, the supervisor should be sure to continuously impress the seriousness of the mistakes upon the subordinate.
    C. When making his criticism, the supervisor should guard against referring to any work that was well done. since this would reduce the effect of his criticism.
    D. The supervisor should focus his criticism on the mistakes being made and should avoid downgrading the subordinate personally.
16._____

17. Of the following, the *BEST* descriptive statement of an effective supervisor is *generally,* that he
    A. works alongside his subordinates on the same type of work
    B. catches all errors when they are made
    C. gives many specific work orders and few general work orders
    D. devotes much of his time to long-range activities, such as planning and improving human relations
17._____

18. When a new method of performing a job operation is to be instituted, the one of the following approaches which will *MOST* generally gain acceptance of the change by subordinates is to
    A. hold a friendly, informal meeting after the change has been implemented to explain the advantages of the new method
    B. consult the subordinates involved in the change as early as possible in the planning stage
    C. work closely with just one of the subordinates who will be affected by the change so that others need not be taken off the job
    D. implement the change, instruct employees fully in the new method, and then follow up on results
18._____

19. Of the following, a supervisor interested in setting quality standards for work produced by his subordinates *PRIMARILY* should   19._____
    A. consult with office supervisors in other organizations to determine the range of acceptable standards
    B. institute a quality improvement program and set standards at the point where quality levels off at desirable levels
    C. establish an ad hoc committee comprised of a representative sample of office workers to set firm and exacting standards
    D. consult the Quality Standards Handbook which predetermines with mathematical precision the level that office quality should meet

20. During a conversation with his supervisor, a subordinate begins to discuss what appears to the supervisor to be a deep-seated personality problem that has been bothering the subordinate. For the supervisor to suggest to the subordinate the possibility of professional help would *NORMALLY* be   20._____
    A. *undesirable;* the necessity of requiring professional help would automatically disqualify the subordinate from being promoted in the future
    B. *desirable;* generally a supervisor can be of limited assistance in personally solving deep-seated personality problems
    C. *undesirable;* since the supervisor was approached by the employee it is his responsibility as a supervisor to help the employee solve his problem
    D. *desirable;* in accordance with the Civil Service Commission regulations a supervisor is not allowed to get involved in subordinates personal problems

21. Of the followings, the supervisory practice which is *LEAST* likely to produce a favorable work environment is that the supervisor   21._____
    A. takes an active interest in subordinates
    B. does not tolerate mistakes regardless of who has made the mistake
    C. gives praise when justified
    D. disciplines individuals in accordance with their violation of the rules

22. Choosing supervisors strictly from within a particular working section *GENERALLY* is   22._____
    A. *desirable,* primarily because the budgeting necessary for promotion is substantially decreased
    B. *undesirable* because personal preferences will always outweigh merit
    C. *desirable* primarily because a good worker within that section will be a good supervisor for that section alone
    D. *undesirable,* primarily because the pool of candidates will be severely limited

23. The chairman of an academic department is currently in conference and has
appointments scheduled for the remainder of the day. He has requested that the
office assistant keep interruptions to a minimum. A caller, who does not have an
appointment and who refuses to identify himself other than to say that he is a student
insists upon seeing the chairman. Of the following, the *MOST* appropriate action to
be taken by the office assistant *generally* would be to
    A. courteously but firmly refuse admittance, and offer to schedule an appointment
for another day
    B. tell the student that he may wait and will probably be able to see the chairman
between other scheduled appointments
    C. ask the student to wait while she consults with the chairman to determine if this is
a legitimate interruption
    D. send the student in to the chairman's office to ask if he may interrupt the
chairman briefly

23._____

24. An office assistant who has been out of her office for an hour returns and notices a
visitor whose presence has apparently not been acknowledged by any of the other
office workers. Of the following, the *MOST* appropriate action for her to take is to
    A. request the office worker seated closest to the front to assist the visitor
    B. return to her desk and wait for one of the other office workers to recognize the
visitor's presence
    C. walk to the middle of the office and announce, "There's a visitor present."
    D. offer assistance to the visitor immediately.

24._____

25. Assume that Dr. Jones, the coordinator of the teacher education program is in
Washington to present a proposal for funding of a research project. During his
absence, a Professor Van Slyke, who identifies himself as a professor from another
university, telephones and asks to speak with Dr. Jones. Of the following, the *MOST*
appropriate reply for the college office assistant to make is:
    A. "He is in Washington, D.C. Please try again tomorrow."
    B. "He is not in the office today he will be back tomorrow morning. May I ask him to
call you then?"
    C. He's on an interview down at the U.S. Office of Education. Is there anything I
might do to assist you ?"
    D. "Please try again tomorrow. Dr. Jones is out seeking funds for our education
research program."

25._____

KEY (CORRECT ANSWERS)

1.	C	11.	C
2.	B	12.	B
3.	B	13.	B
4.	D	14.	B
5.	B	15.	C
6.	A	16.	D
7.	C	17.	D
8.	A	18.	B
9.	A	19.	B
10.	D	20.	B

21.	B
22.	D
23.	A
24.	D
25.	B

EXAMINATION SECTION
TEST 1

DIRECTIONS: Each question or incomplete statement is followed by several suggested
answers or completions. Select the one that BEST answers the question or
completes the statement. *PRINT THE LETTER OF THE CORRECT ANSWER
IN THE SPACE AT THE RIGHT.*

1. You have recently been assigned to a new office and are expected to supervise six   1.____
    clerks.
    All of the following would be good introductory steps to take EXCEPT

    A.   giving a clear presentation of yourself to the clerks, including a short summary of
         your recent work experience
    B.   initiating informal discussions with each clerk concerning his work
    C.   making a general survey of all the functions which each clerk has been performing
    D.   making a list of the duties each clerk is required to perform and giving it to the clerk

2. Your supervisor has advised you that a specific aspect of a job is being done incorrectly   2.____
    and you acknowledge the mistake.
    Of the following, the MOST efficient way of dealing with this situation is to

    A.   call a meeting of the clerks who are performing this particular function and explain
         the correct method
    B.   assume the blame and correct the errors as they are given to you
    C.   speak with each clerk individually and carefully show each one the proper method
    D.   distribute a set of written instructions covering all clerical procedures to the
         employees doing that particular job

3. A new department regulation calls for a change in a particular method of processing new   3.____
    applications. Two clerks have complained to you that the new method is more time-con-
    suming, and they prefer to do it the original way.
    Of the following, what is the MOST advisable thing to do?

    A.   Discuss the situation with them and attempt to determine whether they are utilizing
         the method properly.
    B.   Discuss the advantages of both methods with them and let them use the one that
         is more practical.
    C.   Firmly instruct the clerks to proceed with the new method since it is not up to them
         to refute department policy.
    D.   Tell them to survey the opinions of the other clerks on this matter and inform you of
         the results.

4. A member of the clerical staff has recently begun reporting late for work rather regularly.   4.____
    On each occasion, the individual presented an excuse, but the latenesses continue.
    Of the following, the MOST advisable action for her supervisor to take is to

    A.   have a staff meeting and stress the importance of being on time for work, without
         singling out the specific individual
    B.   put a notice on the departmental office bulletin board, specifying and stressing that
         lateness can not be tolerated

   C.   talk privately with the individual to determine whether there are any unusual circumstances that might be causing the lateness

   D.   send the individual a memorandum clearly indicating that continual lateness will result in disciplinary action

5. Assume that, as the supervisor of a unit, you have been asked to prepare a vacation schedule for your subordinate employees. The employees have had different lengths of service. Some of them have already submitted requests for certain weeks.
Of the following, which factor would be LEAST important in setting up this schedule?

   A.   Your opinion of each employee's past work performance
   B.   Each employee's preference for a vacation period
   C.   The amount of work the unit is expected to accomplish during the vacation period
   D.   The number of employees who have requested to go on vacation at the same time

5._____

6. Your superior finds that he must leave the office one day before he has had time to check and sign the day's correspondence. He asks you to proofread the letters, have corrections made where necessary, and then sign his name. You have never signed his name before.
Of the following, the BEST thing for you to do is to

   A.   sign your superior's name in full, making it look as much like his handwriting as possible
   B.   sign your superior's name and your own name in full as proof that you signed for him
   C.   sign your superior's name in full and add your initials to show that the signature is not his own
   D.   politely refuse to sign his name because it is forgery

6._____

7. The head of your office sometimes makes handwritten notations on original letters which he receives and requests that you mail the letters back to the sender. Of the following, the BEST action for you to take FIRST is to

   A.   request that this practice be stopped because it does not provide for a record in the files
   B.   request that this practice be stopped because it is not the customary way to respond to letters
   C.   photocopy the letters so that there are copies for the file and then send the letters out
   D.   ask the head of your office if he wants you to keep any record of the letters

7._____

8. The main function of most agency administrative offices is *information management*. Information that is received by an administrative office may be classified as active (information which requires the recipient to take some action) or passive (information which does not require action).
Which one of the following items received must clearly be treated as ACTIVE information?
A(n)

   A.   confirmation of payment
   B.   press release concerning an agency event
   C.   advertisement for a new restaurant opening near the agency
   D.   request for a student transcript

8._____

9. Which of the following statements about the use of the photocopy process is COR-
RECT?   9.____

    A. It is difficult to use.
    B. It can be used to reproduce color.
    C. It does not print well on colored paper.
    D. Once source documents have been used, they cannot be used again.

10. In order to get the BEST estimate of how long a repetitive office procedure should take, a   10.____
supervisor should find out how

    A. long it takes her best worker to do the procedure once on a typical day
    B. long it takes her best and worst workers to do the procedure once on a typical day
    C. much time her best worker spends on the procedure during a typical week and the
total number of times the worker executes the procedure during the same week
    D. much time all her subordinates spend on the procedure during a typical week and
the total number of times the procedure was executed during the same week by all
employees

11. Of the following, the MOST suitable and appropriate way to make 250 copies of a partic-   11.____
ular form is to

    A. print all 250 copies on the office computer
    B. delegate the work to someone else
    C. reproduce it on a photocopying machine
    D. use an offset printing process

Questions 12-18.

DIRECTIONS: Questions 12 through 18 are to be answered on the basis of the extracts
shown below from Federal withholding tables. These tables indicate the
amounts which must be withheld from the employee's salary by his employer
for Federal income tax and for social security. They are based on weekly earn-
ings.

INCOME TAX WITHHOLDING TABLE

The wages are -		And the number of withholding exemptions claimed is-					
At least	But less than	0	1	2	3	4	5
		The amount of income tax to be withheld shall be -					
$200	$205	$14.10	$11.80	$ 9.50	$ 7.20	$ 4.90	$2.80
205	210	14.90	12.60	10.30	8.00	5.70	3.50
210	215	15.70	13.40	11.10	8.80	6.50	4.20
215	220	16.50	14.20	11.90	9.60	7.30	5.00
220	225	17.30	15.00	12.70	10.40	8.10	5.80
225	230	18.10	15.80	13.50	11.20	8.90	6.60
230	235	18.90	16.60	14.30	12.00	9.70	7.40
235	240	19.70	17.40	15.10	12.80	10.50	8.20
240	245	20.50	18.20	15.90	13.60	11.30	9.00
245	250	21.30	19.00	16.70	14.40	12.10	9.80

SOCIAL SECURITY EMPLOYEE TAX TABLE

Wages		Tax to be withheld	Wages		Tax to be withheld
At least	But less than		At least	But less than	
$202.79	$202.99	$15.35	$229.72	$229.91	$16.75
202.99	203.18	15.36	229.91	230.10	16.76
203.18	203.37	15.37	230.10	230.29	16.77
203.37	203.56	15.38	230.29	230.49	16.78
203.56	203.75	15.39	230.49	230.68	16.79
203.75	203.95	15.40	230.68	230.87	16.80
203.95	204.14	15.41	230.87	231.06	16.81
204.14	204.33	15.42	231.06	231.25	16.82
204.33	204.52	15.43	231.25	231.45	16.83
204.52	204.72	15.44	231.45	231.64	16.84

Wages		Tax to be withheld	Wages		Tax to be withheld
At least	But less than		At least	But less than	
$222.02	$222.22	$16.35	$234.52	$234.72	$17.00
222.22	222.41	16.36	234.72	234.91	17.01
222.41	222.60	16.37	234.91	235.10	17.02
222.60	222.79	16.38	235.10	235.29	17.03
222.79	222.99	16.39	235.29	235.49	17.04
222.99	223.18	16.40	235.49	235.68	17.05
223.18	223.37	16.41	235.68	235.87	17.06
223.37	223.56	16.42	235.87	236.06	17.07
223.56	223.75	16.43	236.06	236.25	17.08
223.75	223.95	16.44	236.25	236.45	17.09

12. Dave Andes has wages of $242.75 for one week. He has claimed three withholding   12.____
    exemptions.
    What is the Federal income tax which should be withheld?

    A. $13.60   B. $15.90   C. $18.20   D. $20.50

13. Mary Hodes has wages of $229.95 for one week.   13.____
    What is the Social Security tax which should be withheld?

    A. $16.75   B. $16.76   C. $16.77   D. $16.78

14. Joe Jones had wages of $235.63 for one week. He has claimed two withholding exemp-   14.____
    tions.
    What is the Federal income tax which should be withheld?

    A. $12.80   B. $14.30   C. $15.10   D. $17.40

15. Tom Stein had wages of $203.95 for one week. What is the Social Security tax which   15.____
    should be withheld?

    A. $15.40   B. $15.41   C. $16.05   D. $16.06

16. Robert Helman had wages of $222.80 for one week. He has claimed one withholding   16.____
    exemption.
    If only Federal income tax and Social Security tax were deducted from his earnings for
    the same week, how much *take-home* pay should he have for the week?

    A. $191.41   B. $193.96   C. $194.12   D. $195.65

17. Audrey Stein has wages of $203.00 for one week. She claimed no withholding exemp-   17.____
    tions.
    If only Federal income tax and Social Security tax were deducted from her earnings for
    the same week, how much *take-home* pay should she have for the week?

    A. $171.84   B. $172.34   C. $173.54   D. $175.84

18. Anthony Covallo, who worked 28 hours in the past week, has a regular hourly rate of   18.____
    $7.25 per hour and earns a premium of time and a half for hours over 40. He has claimed
    four withholding exemptions.
    After Social Security tax and Federal income tax are deducted from his wages for the
    past week, how much pay does he have left?

    A. $180.98   B. $181.13   C. $182.29   D. $182.74

19. In judging the adequacy of a standard office form, which of the following is LEAST impor-   19.____
    tant?
    _____ of the form.

    A. Date   B. Legibility   C. Size   D. Design

20. Clear and accurate telephone messages should be taken for employees who are out of   20.____
    the office.
    Which of the following is of LEAST importance when taking a telephone message?

    A. Name of the person called
    B. Name of the caller

C. Details of the message
D. Time of the call

21. Suppose that all office supplies are kept in a centrally located cabinet in the office. Of the following, which is usually the BEST policy to adhere to for distribution of supplies?

   A. Permit employees to stock up on all supplies to avoid frequent trips to the cabinet.
   B. Assign one employee to be in charge of distributing all supplies to other employees at frequent intervals.
   C. Inform employees that supplies should be taken in large quantities and only when needed.
   D. Keep cabinet closed and instruct employees that they must check with you before taking supplies.

21.____

Questions 22-25.

DIRECTIONS: Questions 22 through 25 are to be answered SOLELY on the basis of the following passage.

Use of the systems and procedures approach to office management is revolutionizing the supervision of office work. This approach views an enterprise as an entity which seeks to fulfill definite objectives. Systems and procedures help to organize repetitive work into a routine, thus reducing the amount of decision-making required for its accomplishment. As a result, employees are guided in their efforts and perform only necessary work. Supervisors are relieved of any details of execution and are free to attend to more important work. Establishing work guides which require that identical tasks be performed the same way each, time permits standardization of forms, machine operations, work methods, and controls. This approach also reduces the probability of errors. Any error committed is usually discovered quickly because the incorrect work does not meet the requirement of the work guides. Errors are also reduced through work specialization which allows each employee to become thoroughly proficient in a particular type of work. Such proficiency also tends to improve the morale of the employees.

22. Of the following, which one BEST expresses the main theme of the above passage? The

   A. advantages and disadvantages of the systems and procedures approach to office management
   B. effectiveness of the systems and procedures approach to office management in developing skills
   C. systems and procedures approach to office management as it relates to office costs
   D. advantages of the systems and procedures approach to office management for supervisors and office workers

22.____

23. Work guides are LEAST likely to be used when

   A. standardized forms are used
   B. a particular office task is distinct and different from all others
   C. identical tasks are to be performed in identical ways
   D. similar work methods are expected from each employee

23.____

14

24. According to the above passage, when an employee makes a work error, it USUALLY   24.____

    A. is quickly corrected by the supervisor
    B. necessitates a change in the work guides
    C. can be detected quickly if work guides are in use
    D. increases the probability of further errors by that employee

25. The above passage states that the accuracy of an employee's work is INCREASED by   25.____

    A. using the work specialization approach
    B. employing a probability sample
    C. requiring him to shift at one time into different types of tasks
    D. having his supervisor check each detail of work execution

---

KEY (CORRECT ANSWERS)

1.	D		11.	C
2.	A		12.	A
3.	A		13.	B
4.	C		14.	C
5.	A		15.	B
6.	C		16.	A
7.	D		17.	C
8.	D		18.	D
9.	B		19.	A
10.	D		20.	D

21.	B
22.	D
23.	B
24.	C
25.	A

15

TEST 2

Each question or incomplete statement is followed by several suggested answers or completions. Select the one that BEST answers the question or completes the statement. *PRINT THE LETTER OF THE CORRECT ANSWER IN THE SPACE AT THE RIGHT.*

1. A certain supervisor often holds group meetings with subordinates to discuss the goals of the unit and manpower requirements for meeting objectives.
   For the supervisor to hold such meetings is a

   A. *good* practice because it will aid both the supervisor and subordinates in planning and completing the unit's work
   B. *good* practice because it will prevent future problems from interfering with the unit's objectives
   C. *poor* practice because the supervisor has the sole responsibility for meeting objectives and should make manpower decisions without any advice
   D. *poor* practice because the subordinates will be allowed to set their own work quotas

   1.____

2. Assume that you are a supervisor who has been asked to evaluate the work of a clerk who was transferred to your unit about six months ago.
   Which one of the following, by itself, provides the BEST basis for making such an evaluation?

   A. Ask the clerk's former supervisor about the employee's previous work.
   B. Ask the clerk's co-workers for their opinions of the employee's work.
   C. Evaluate the quantity and quality of the employee's work over the six-month period.
   D. Observe the employee's performance from time to time during the next week and base your evaluation on these observations.

   2.____

3. Which of the following would be the MOST desirable way for a supervisor to help improve the job performance of a particular subordinate?

   A. Criticize the employee's performance in front of other employees.
   B. Privately warn the employee that failure to meet work standards may lead to dismissal.
   C. Hold a meeting with this employee and other subordinates in which the need to improve the unit's performance is stressed.
   D. Meet privately with the employee and discuss both positive and negative aspects of the employee's work

   3.____

4. Suppose that your office has a limited supply of a pamphlet which people may read in your office when they seek certain information, but another office in your building is supposed to have a large supply available for distribution to the public.
   Which of the following would be the BEST thing for you to do when someone states that he has not been able to obtain one of these pamphlets?

   A. Tell him that he misunderstood the directions that other employees have given him and carefully direct him to the other office.
   B. Ask whether he has visited the other office and requested a copy from them.
   C. Let him take one of your office's copies of the pamphlet and then call the other office and ask why they have run out of copies for distribution.

   4.____

D. Tell him that your office does its best to keep the public informed but that this might not be true of other offices.

5. On Monday, a clerk made many errors in completing a new daily record form. The supervisor explained the errors and had the clerk correct the form. On Tuesday, the clerk made fewer errors. Because he was very busy, the supervisor did not point out the errors to the clerk but corrected the errors himself. On Wednesday, the clerk made the same number of errors as on Tuesday. The supervisor reprimanded the clerk for making so many errors.   5.____

The supervisor's handling of this situation on Wednesday may be considered poor MAINLY because the

A. clerk was not given enough time to complete each form properly
B. supervisor should not have expected improvement without further training
C. clerk was obviously incapable of completing the form
D. supervisor should have continued to correct the errors himself

Questions 6-8.

DIRECTIONS: Questions 6 through 8 are to be answered SOLELY on the basis of the information contained in the following passage.

When using words like company, association, council, committee, and board in place of the full official name, the writer should not capitalize these short forms unless he intends them to invoke the full force of the institution's authority. In legal contracts, in minutes, or in formal correspondence where one is speaking formally and officially on behalf of the company, the term "Company" is usually capitalized, but in ordinary usage, where it is not essential to load the short form with this significance, capitalization would be excessive. (Example: The company will have many good openings for graduates this June.)

The treatment recommended for short forms of place names is essentially the same as that recommended for short forms of organizational names. In general, we capitalize the full form but not the short form. If Park Avenue is referred to in one sentence, then "the avenue" is sufficient in subsequent references. The same is true with words like building, hotel, station, and airport, which are capitalized when part of a proper name (Pan Am Building, Hotel Plaza, Union Station, O'Hare Airport) but are simply lower-cased when replacing these specific names.

6. The above passage states that USUALLY the short forms of names of organizations   6.____

A. and places should not be capitalized
B. and places should be capitalized
C. should not be capitalized, but the short forms of names of places should be capitalized
D. should be capitalized, but the short forms of names of places should not be capitalized

7. The above passage states that in legal contracts, in minutes, and in formal correspondence, the short forms of names of organizations should   7.____

A. usually not be capitalized
B. usually be capitalized
C. usually not be used
D. never be used

8. It can be INFERRED from the above passage that decisions regarding when to capitalize   8.____
   certain words

   A. should be left to the discretion of the writer
   B. should be based on generally accepted rules
   C. depend on the total number of words capitalized
   D. are of minor importance

9. The Central Terminal and the Gardens Terminal are located on Glover Street.   9.____
   In ordinary usage, if this sentence were to be followed by the sentence in the choices
   below, which form of the sentence would be CORRECT?

   A. Both Terminals are situated on the same street.
   B. Both terminals are situated on the same Street.
   C. Both terminals are situated on the same street.
   D. Both Terminals are situated on the same Street.

10. A stylus is a(n)   10.____

   A. implement for writing containing a cylinder of graphite
   B. implement for writing with ink or a similar fluid
   C. pointed implement used to write
   D. stick of colored wax used for writing

11. As a supervisor, you have the responsibility of teaching new employees the functions   11.____
   and procedures of your office after their orientation by the personnel office.
   Of the following, the BEST way to begin such instruction is to

   A. advise the new employee of the benefits and services available to him, over and
      above his salary
   B. discuss the negative aspects of the departmental procedures and indicate meth-
      ods available to overcome them
   C. assist the new employee in understanding the general purpose of the office proce-
      dures and how they fit in with the overall operation
   D. give a detailed briefing of the operations of your office, its functions and procedures

12. Assume that you are the supervisor of a clerical unit. One of the duties of the employees   12.____
   in your unit is to conduct a brief interview with persons using the services of your agency
   for the first time. The purpose of the interview is to get general background information in
   order to best direct them to the appropriate division.
   A clerk comes to your office and says that a prospective client has just called her some
   rather unpleasant names, accused her of being nosey and meddlesome, and has
   stated emphatically that she refuses to talk with an *underling,* meaning the clerk. The
   young woman is almost in tears. Of the following, what is the FIRST action you should
   take?

   A. Immediately call the agency's protection officer, have him advise the client of the
      regulations, and tell her that she will be removed if she is not more polite.
   B. Calm the clerk, introduce yourself to the client, and quietly discuss the agency's
      services, regulations, and informational needs, and request that she complete the
      interview with the clerk.

C.   Calm the clerk, have her return and firmly advise the client of the agency's rules concerning the need for this first interview.

D.   Introduce yourself to the client and advise her that without an apology to the clerk and completion of the interview, she will not be given any service.

13.   A recent high school graduate has just been assigned to the unit which you supervise. Which of the following would be the LEAST desirable technique to use with this employee?   13.____

A.   At any one time, give the new employee only as much detail about the job as the employee can absorb.

B.   Always tell the new employee the correct procedure, then demonstrate how it is accomplished.

C.   Assign the employee the same quantity and type of work that the other employees are doing to see if the employee can handle the job.

D.   Assume the employee is tense and be prepared to repeat procedures and descriptions.

14.   Assume that you supervise a work unit of several employees. Which of the following is LEAST essential in assuring that the goals which you set for the unit are achieved?   14.____

A.   Establishing objectives and standards for the staff
B.   Providing justification for disciplinary action
C.   Measuring performance or progress of individuals against standards
D.   Taking corrective action where performance is less than expected

15.   One of the clerks you supervise is often reluctant to accept assignments and usually complains about the amount of work expected, although the other clerks with the same assignments and workload seem quite happy.
Of the following, the MOST accurate assumption that you can make about this clerk is that she   15.____

A.   will require additional observation and help
B.   will eventually have to be discharged or transferred
C.   is incompetent
D.   is overworked

Questions 16-21.

DIRECTIONS: Questions 16 through 21 are to be answered SOLELY on the basis of the airline timetable and the information appearing on the last page of this test.

Fact Situation:
An administrator wants you to purchase airline tickets for him so that he can attend a meeting being held in Chicago on Monday. He must leave from LaGuardia Airport in New York on Monday morning as late as possible but with arrival in Chicago no later than 9:00 A.M. He wishes to fly coach/economy class both ways. The meeting is due to end at 5:30 P.M., and he wishes to obtain the first plane after 6:45 P.M. going back to LaGuardia Airport. If all these requirements have been met, he would, if possible, also like to fly to and leave from Midway Airport in Chicago and go non-stop both ways.

16. You should obtain a ticket for the administrator from New York to Chicago on flight number   16._____
    ber

    A. 483   B. 201   C. 277   D. 539

17. You should obtain a ticket for the administrator from Chicago to New York on flight number   17._____
    ber

    A. 588   B. 692   C. 268   D. 334

18. The administrator decides to take limousines to and from both airports.   18._____
    If the limousine charge in Chicago is $52.50. and there is no reduced rate for a round-
    trip flight, what is the cost of the administrator's round-trip air fare PLUS limousine ser-
    vice?

    A. $827.50   B. $931.00   C. $963.00   D. $967.00

19. The administrator asked you whether he would be able to get breakfast on his flight to   19._____
    Chicago or whether he should go to the airport early and eat there before boarding the
    plane. He prefers to eat on the plane.
    Of the following, the BEST reply to make is:

    A. I will have to telephone the airport to find out
    B. You should eat at the airport
    C. A meal is served on the plane
    D. Only certain passengers get a meal on the plane

20. Of the following requests of the administrator concerning his travel arrangements, which   20._____
    one is IMPOSSIBLE to meet?

    A. Chicago arrival no later than 9 A.M.
    B. New York departure from LaGuardia Airport
    C. Non-stop flights both ways
    D. Chicago departure from Midway Airport

21. Suppose that it is necessary to take a first-class seat on the trip to Chicago although you   21._____
    have no problem reserving a coach/economy seat on the return trip.
    If there is no reduction in fare for round-trip flights, how much MORE will this trip cost
    than round-trip coach/ economy?

    A. $209   B. $236   C. $318   D. $636

22. Ms. X, a clerk under your supervision, has been working in the unit for a few weeks.   22._____
    Some of the other employees have complained to you that Ms. X has an annoying habit
    of constantly tapping her feet on the floor and it disturbs their work.
    The BEST thing for you to do is to

    A. ignore the complaints because the employees should be concerned only with their
        own habits
    B. speak with Ms. X privately and discuss the situation with her
    C. make a general announcement that employees should control their nervous habits
    D. observe Ms. X for a few weeks to see if the employees are correct, and then take
        action

23. Suppose you answer a telephone call from someone who states that he is a friend of one of your co-workers and needs the employee's new address in order to send an invitation. Your co-worker is on vacation but you know her address.
Which of the following is the BEST action for you to take?

    A. Give the caller the address but ask the caller not to mention that you are the one who gave it out.
    B. Give the caller the address and leave a note for your co-worker stating what you did.
    C. Tell the caller you do not know the address but will give the employee's phone number if that will help.
    D. Offer to take his name and address and have your co-worker contact him.

23.____

24. Assume that you receive a telephone call in which the caller requests information which you know is posted in the office next to yours. You start to tell the caller you will transfer her call to the right office, but she interrupts you and says she has been transferred from office to office and is tired of getting a *run-around*. Of the following, the BEST thing for you to do is to

    A. give the caller the phone number of the office next to yours and quickly end the conversation
    B. give her the phone number of the office next to yours and tell her you will try to transfer her call
    C. ask her if she wants to hold on while you get the information for her
    D. tell the caller that she could have avoided the *run-around* by asking for the right office, and suggest that she come in person

24.____

25. Assume that your unit processes confidential forms which are submitted by persons seeking financial assistance. An individual comes to your office, gives you his name, and states that he would like to look over a form which he sent in about a week ago because he believes he omitted some important information.
Of the following, the BEST thing for you to do FIRST is to

    A. locate the proper form
    B. call the individual's home telephone number to verify his identity
    C. ask the individual if he has proof of his identity
    D. call the security office

25.____

KEY (CORRECT ANSWERS)

1.	A	11.	C
2.	C	12.	B
3.	D	13.	C
4.	B	14.	B
5.	B	15.	A
6.	A	16.	A
7.	B	17.	D
8.	B	18.	B
9.	C	19.	C
10.	C	20.	D

21.	C
22.	B
23.	D
24.	C
25.	C

———

EXAMINATION SECTION
TEST 1

DIRECTIONS: Each question or incomplete statement is followed by several suggested answers or completions. Select the one that BEST answers the question or completes the statement. *PRINT THE LETTER OF THE CORRECT ANSWER IN THE SPACE AT THE RIGHT.*

1. When you select someone to serve as supervisor of your unit during your absence on vacation and at other times, it would generally be BEST to choose the employee who is

   A. able to move the work along smoothly without friction
   B. on staff longest
   C. liked best by the rest of the staff
   D. able to perform the work of each employee to be supervised

1.____

2. Successful supervision of handicapped persons employed in a department depends MOST on providing them with a work place and work climate

   A. which is safe and accident-free
   B. that requires close and direct supervision by others
   C. that requires the performance of routine, repetitive tasks under a minimum of pressure
   D. where they will be accepted by the other employees

2.____

3. Studies have indicated that when employees feel that their work is aimless and unchallenging, the allocation or payment of more money for this type of work is LIKELY to

   A. contribute little to increased production
   B. bring more status to this work
   C. increase employees' feelings of security
   D. give employees greater motivation

3.____

4. An employee's performance has fallen below established minimum standards of quantity and quality.
   The threat of monetary or other disciplinary action as a device for improving this employee's performance would PROBABLY be acceptable and most effective

   A. only if applied as soon as the performance fell below standard
   B. only after more constructive techniques have failed
   C. at any time provided the employee understands that the punishment will be carried out
   D. at no time

4.____

5. A supervisor must, on short notice, ask his staff to work overtime.
   Of the following, a technique that is MOST likely to win their willing cooperation would be to

   A. explain that occasional overtime is part of the job requirement
   B. explain that they will be doing him a personal favor which he will appreciate very much
   C. explain why the overtime is necessary
   D. promise them that they can take the extra time off in the near future

5.____

6. On checking a completed work assignment of an employee, the supervisor finds that the work was not done correctly because the employee had not understood his instructions. Of the following, the BEST way to prevent repetition of this situation next time is for the supervisor to

    6.____

    A. ask the employee whether he fully understood the instructions and tell him to ask questions in the future whenever anything is unclear
    B. ask the employee to repeat the instructions given and test his understanding with several key questions
    C. give the instructions a second time, emphasizing the more complicated aspects of the job
    D. give work instructions in writing

7. If, as a supervisor, you find yourself pressured for time to handle all of your job responsibilities, the one of the following tasks which it would be MOST appropriate for you to delegate to a subordinate is

    7.____

    A. attending a staff conference of unit supervisors to discuss the implementation of a new departmental policy
    B. making staff work assignments
    C. interviewing a new employee
    D. checking work of certain employees for accuracy

8. Suppose you are unavoidably late for work one morning. When you arrive at 10 o'clock, you find there are several matters demanding your attention.
Which one of the following matters should you handle LAST?

    8.____

    A. A visitor who had a 9:30 appointment with you has been waiting to see you since 9 o'clock
    B. An employee on an assignment which should have been completed that morning is absent, and the work will have to be reassigned
    C. Several letters which you dictated at the end of the previous day have been typed and are on your desk for signature and mailing
    D. Your superior called asking you to get certain information for him when you come in and to call him back

9. Suppose that you have assigned a typist to type a report containing considerable statistical and tabular material and have given her specific instructions as to how this material is to be laid out on each page. When she returns the completed report, you find that it was not prepared according to your instructions, but you may possibly be able to use it the way it was typed. When you question her, she states that she thought her layout was better, but you were unavailable for consultation when she began the work.
Of the following, the BEST action for you to take is to

    9.____

    A. criticize her for not doing the work according to your instructions
    B. have her retype the report
    C. praise her for her work but tell her she could have waited until she could consult you
    D. praise her for using initiative

10. Of the following, the MOST effective way for a supervisor to correct poor working habits of an employee which result in low and poor quality output is to give the employee

    10.____

24

A.   additional training
B.   less demanding assignments until his work improves
C.   continuous supervision
D.   more severe criticism

11.   Of the following, the BEST way for a supervisor to teach an employee how to do a new   11.____
and somewhat complicated job is to

    A.   assign him to observe another employee who is already skilled in this work and
instruct him to consult this employee if he has any questions
    B.   explain to him how to do it, then demonstrate how it is done, then observe and cor-
rect the employee as he does it, then follow up
    C.   give him a written, detailed, step-by-step explanation of how to do the job and
instruct him to ask questions if anything is unclear when he does the work
    D.   teach him the easiest part of the job first, then the other parts one at a time, in
order of their difficulty, as the employee masters the easier parts

12.   After an employee has completed telling his supervisor about a grievance against a co-   12.____
worker, the supervisor tells the employee that he will take action to remove the cause of
the grievance.
The action of the supervisor was

    A.   *good* because ill feeling between subordinates interferes with proper performance
    B.   *poor* because the supervisor should give both employees time to *cool off*
    C.   *good* because grievances that appear petty to the supervisor are important to sub-
ordinates
    D.   *poor* because the supervisor should tell the employee that he will investigate the
matter before he comes to any conclusion

13.   During work on an important project, one employee in a secretarial pool turns in several   13.____
pages of typed copy, one page of which contains several errors.
Of these four comments which her supervisor might possibly make, which one would
be MOST constructive?

    A.   "You did such a poor job on this; I 'll have to have it done over."
    B.   "You will have to do better more consistently than this if you want to be in charge of
a secretarial pool yourself someday."
    C.   "How come you made so many mistakes here? Your other pages were all right."
    D.   "If my boss saw this, he'd be very displeased with you."

14.   A supervisor has general supervision over a large, complex project with many employ-   14.____
ees. The work is subdivided among small units of employees, each with a senior clerk or
senior stenographer in charge. At a staff meeting, after all work assignments have been
made, the supervisor tells all the employees that they are to take orders only from their
immediate supervisor and instructs them to let him know if any one else tries to give
them orders.
This instruction by the supervisor is

    A.   *good* because it may prevent the issuance of orders by unauthorized persons
which would interfere with the accomplishment of the assignment
    B.   *poor* because employees should be instructed to take up such problems with their
immediate supervisor

C. *good* because orders issued by immediate supervisors would be precise and directly related to the tasks of the assignments while those issued by others would not be
D. *poor* because it places upon all employees a responsibility which should not normally be theirs

15. A supervisor who is to direct a team of senior clerks and clerks and senior stenographers and stenographers in a complex project calls them together beforehand to inform them of the tasks each employee will perform on this job. Of the following, the CHIEF value of this action by the supervisor is that each member of this team will be able to   15.____

A. work independently in the absence of the supervisor
B. understand what he will do and how this will fit into the total picture
C. share in the process of decision-making as an equal participant
D. judge how well the plans for this assignment have been made

16. A supervisor who has both younger and older employees under his supervision may sometimes find that employee absenteeism seriously interferes with accomplishment of goals.   16.____
Studies of such employee absenteeism have shown that the absences of employees

A. under 35 years of age are usually unexpected and the absences of employees over 45 years of age are usually unnecessary
B. of all age groups show the same characteristics as to length of absence
C. under 35 years of age are for frequent, short periods while the absences of employees over 45 years of age are less frequent but of longer duration
D. under 35 years of age are for periods of long duration and the absences of employees over 45 years of age are for periods of short duration

17. Suppose you have a long-standing procedure for getting a certain job done by your subordinates that is apparently a good one. Changes in some steps of the procedure are made from time to time to handle special problems that come up.   17.____
For you to review this procedure periodically is desirable MAINLY because

A. the system is working well
B. checking routines periodically is a supervisor's chief responsibility
C. subordinates may be confused as to how the procedure operates as a result of the changes made
D. it is necessary to determine whether the procedure has become outdated or is in need of improvement

18. In conducting an interview, the BEST types of questions with which to begin the interview are those which the person interviewed is _____ to answer.   18.____

A. willing and able   B. willing but unable
C. able to but unwilling   D. unable and unwilling

19. In order to determine accurately a child's age, it is BEST for an interviewer to rely on   19.____

A. the child's grade in school   B. what the mother says
C. birth records   D. a library card

20. In his first interview with a new employee, it would be LEAST appropriate for a unit super-   20.____
visor to

    A.   find out the employee's preference for the several types of jobs to which he is able
to assign him
    B.   determine whether the employee will make good promotion material
    C.   inform the employee of what his basic job responsibilities will be
    D.   inquire about the employee's education and previous employment

21. If an interviewer takes care to phrase his questions carefully and precisely, the result will   21.____
MOST probably be that

    A.   he will be able to determine whether the person interviewed is being truthful
    B.   the free flow of the interview will be lost
    C.   he will get the information he wants
    D.   he will ask stereotyped questions and narrow the scope of the interview

22. When, during an interview, is the person interviewed LEAST likely to be cautious about   22.____
what he tells the interviewer?

    A.   Shortly after the beginning when the questions normally suggest pleasant associa-
tions to the person interviewed
    B.   As long as the interviewer keeps his questions to the point
    C.   At the point where the person interviewed gains a clear insight into the area being
discussed
    D.   When the interview appears formally ended and goodbyes are being said

23. In an interview held for the purpose of getting information from the person interviewed, it   23.____
is sometimes desirable for the interviewer to repeat the answer he has received
to a question.
For the interviewer to rephrase such an answer in his own words is good practice
MAINLY because it

    A.   gives the interviewer time to make up his next question
    B.   gives the person interviewed a chance to correct any possible misunderstanding
    C.   gives the person interviewed the feeling that the interviewer considers his answer
important
    D.   prevents the person interviewed from changing his answer

24. There are several methods of formulating questions during an interview. The particular   24.____
method used should be adapted to the interview problems presented by the person
being questioned.
Of the following methods of formulating questions during an interview, the ACCEPT-
ABLE one is for the interviewer to ask questions which

    A.   incorporate several items in order to allow a cooperative interviewee freedom to
organize his statements
    B.   are ambiguous in order to foil a distrustful interviewee
    C.   suggest the correct answer in order to assist an interviewee who appears confused
    D.   would help an otherwise unresponsive interviewee to become more responsive

25. For an interviewer to permit the person being interviewed to read the data the interviewer writes as he records the person's responses on a routine departmental form is   25.____

    A. *desirable* because it serves to assure the person interviewed that his responses are being recorded accurately
    B. *undesirable* because it prevents the interviewer from clarifying uncertain points by asking additional questions
    C. *desirable* because it makes the time that the person interviewed must wait while the answer is written seem shorter
    D. *undesirable* because it destroys the confidentiality of the interview

26. Suppose that a stranger enters the office you are in charge of and asks for the address and telephone number of one of your employees.   26.____
    Of the following, it would be BEST for you to

    A. find out why he needs the information and release it if his reason is a good one
    B. explain that you are not permitted to release such information to unauthorized persons
    C. give him the information but tell him it must be kept confidential
    D. ask him to leave the office immediately

27. A member of the public approaches an employee who is at work at his desk. The employee cannot interrupt his work in order to take care of this person.   27.____
    Of the following, the BEST and MOST courteous way of handling this situation is for the employee to

    A. avoid looking up from his work until he is finished with what he is doing
    B. tell this person that he will not be able to take care of him for quite a while
    C. refer the individual to another employee who can take care of him right away
    D. chat with the individual while he continues with his work

28. You answer a phone call from a citizen who urgently needs certain information you do not have, but you think you know who may have it. He is angry because he has already been switched to two different offices.   28.____
    Of the following, it would be BEST for you to

    A. give him the phone number of the person you think may have the information he wants, but explain you are not sure
    B. tell him you regret you cannot help him because you are not sure who can give him the information
    C. advise him that the best way he can be sure of getting the information he wants is to write a letter to the agency
    D. get the phone number where he can be reached and tell him you will try to get the information he wants and will call him back later

29. Persons who have business with an agency often complain about the *red tape* which complicates or slows up what they are trying to accomplish.   29.____
    As a supervisor of a unit which deals with the public, the LEAST effective of the following actions which you could take to counteract this feeling on the part of a person who has business with your office is to

    A. assure him that your office will make every effort to take care of his matter as fast as possible
    B. tell him that because of the volume of work in your agency he must be patient with *red tape*

    C. give him a reasonable date by which action on the matter he is concerned about will be completed and tell him to call you if he hasn't heard by then

    D. give him an understanding of why the procedures he must comply with are necessary

30. If a receptionist is sorting letters at her desk and a caller appears to make an inquiry, the receptionist should   30._____

    A. ask the caller to have a seat and wait

    B. speak to the caller while continuing the sorting, looking up occasionally

    C. stop what she is doing and give undivided attention to the caller

    D. continue with the sorting until a logical break in the work is reached, then answer any inquiries

31. To avoid cutting off parts of letters when using an automatic letter opener, it is BEST to   31._____

    A. arrange all of the letters so that the addresses are right side up

    B. hold the envelopes up to the light to make sure their contents have not settled to the side that is to be opened

    C. strike the envelopes against a table or desk top several times so that the contents of all the envelopes settle to one side

    D. check the enclosures periodically to make sure that the machine has not been cutting into them

32. Requests to repair office equipment which appears to be unsafe should be given priority MAINLY because if repairs are delayed   32._____

    A. there may be injuries to staff

    B. there may be further deterioration of the equipment

    C. work flow may be interrupted

    D. the cost of repair may increase

33. Of the following types of documents, it is MOST important to retain and file   33._____

    A. working drafts of reports that have been submitted in final form

    B. copies of letters of good will which conveyed a message that could not be handled by phone

    C. interoffice orders for materials which have been received and verified

    D. interoffice memoranda regarding the routing of standard forms

34. Of the following, the BEST reason for discarding certain material from office files would be that the   34._____

    A. files are crowded

    B. material in the files is old

    C. material duplicates information obtainable from other sources in the files

    D. material is referred to most often by employees in an adjoining office

35. Of the following, the BEST reason for setting up a partitioned work area for the typists in your office is that   35._____

    A. an uninterrupted flow of work among the typists will be possible

    B. complaints about ventilation and lighting will be reduced

    C. the first-line supervisor will have more direct control over the typists

    D. the noise of the typewriters will be less disturbing to other workers

36. Of the following, the MAIN factor contributing to the expense of maintaining an office procedure manual would be the
    36.____

    A. infrequent use of the manual
    B. need to revise it regularly
    C. cost of looseleaf binders
    D. high cost of printing

37. From the viewpoint of use of a typewriter to fill in a form, the MOST important design factor to consider is
    37.____

    A. standard spacing
    B. box headings
    C. serial numbering
    D. vertical guide lines

38. Out-of-date and seldom used records should be removed PERIODICALLY from the files because
    38.____

    A. overall responsibility for records will be transferred to the person in charge of the central storage files
    B. duplicate copies of every record are not needed
    C. valuable filing space will be regained and the time needed to find a current record will be cut down
    D. worthwhile suggestions on improving the filing system will result whenever this is done

39. In a certain office, file folders are constantly being removed from the files for use by administrators. At the same time, new material is coming in to be filed in some of these folders.
    39.____
    Of the following, the BEST way to avoid delays in filing of the new material and to keep track of the removed folders is to

    A. keep a sheet listing all folders removed from the file, who has them, and a follow-up date to check on their return; attach to this list new material received for filing
    B. put an *out* slip in the place of any file folder removed, telling what folder is missing, date removed, and who has it; file new material received at front of files
    C. put a temporary *out* folder in place of the one removed, giving title or subject, date removed, and who has it; put into this temporary folder any new material received
    D. keep a list of all folders removed and who has them; forward any new material received for filing while a folder is out to the person who has it

40. Folders labeled *Miscellaneous* should be used in an alphabetic filing system MAINLY to
    40.____

    A. provide quick access to recent material
    B. avoid setting up individual folders for all infrequent correspondents
    C. provide temporary storage for less important documents
    D. temporarily hold papers which will not fit into already crowded individual folders

41. Suppose that one of the office machines in your unit is badly in need of replacement. Of the following, the MOST important reason for postponing immediate purchase of a new machine would be that
    41.____

    A. a later model of the machine is expected on the market in a few months
    B. the new machine is more expensive than the old machine
    C. the operator of the present machine will have to be instructed by the manufacturer in the operation of the new machine
    D. the employee operating the old machine is not complaining

42. If the four steps listed below for processing records were given in logical sequence, the one that would be the THIRD step is: 42.____

    A. Coding the records, using a chart or classification system
    B. Inspecting the records to make sure they have been released for filing
    C. Preparing cross-reference sheets or cards
    D. Skimming the records to determine filing captions

43. The suggestion that memos or directives which circulate among subordinates be initialed by each employee is a   43.____

    A. *poor* one because, with modern copying machines, it should be possible to supply every subordinate with a copy of each message for his personal use
    B. *good* one because it relieves the supervisor of blame for the action of subordinates who have read and initialed the messages
    C. *poor* one because initialing the memo or directive is no guarantee that the subordinate has read the material
    D. *good* one because it can be used as a record by the supervisor to show that his subordinates have received the message and were responsible for reading it

44. Of the following, the MOST important reason for microfilming office records is to   44.____

    A. save storage space needed to keep records
    B. make it easier to get records when needed
    C. speed up the classification of information
    D. shorten the time which records must be kept

45. Your office filing cabinets have become so overcrowded that it is difficult to use the files. Of the following, the MOST desirable step for you to take FIRST to relieve this situation would be to   45.____

    A. assign your assistant to spend some time each day reviewing the material in the files and to give you his recommendations as to what material may be discarded
    B. discard all material which has been in the files more than a given number of years
    C. submit a request for additional filing cabinets in your next budget request
    D. transfer enough material to the central storage room of your agency to give you the amount of additional filing space needed

46. Of the following, the USUAL order of the subdivisions in a standard published report is: 46.____

    A. Table of contents, body of report, index, appendix
    B. Index, table of contents, body of report, appendix
    C. Index, body of report, table of contents, appendix
    D. Table of contents, body of report, appendix, index

47. The BEST type of pictorial illustration to show the approximate percentage breakdown of the titles of employees in a department would be the   47.____

    A. flow chart   B. bar graph
    C. organization chart   D. line graph

48. You are reviewing a draft, written by one of your subordinates, of a report that is to be dis-   48._____
tributed to every bureau and division of your department.
Which one of the following would be the LEAST desirable characteristic of such a
report?

   A. It gives information, explanations, conclusions, and recommendations for which
   purpose it was written.
   B. There is sufficient objective data presented to substantiate the conclusions
   reached and the recommendations made by the writer.
   C. The writing style and opinions of the writer are persuasive enough to win over to its
   conclusions those who read the report, although little data is given in support.
   D. It will be understood easily by the people to whom it will be distributed.

49. According to accepted practice, a business letter is addressed to an organization but   49._____
marked for the attention of a specific individual whenever the sender wants

   A. only the person to whose attention the letter is sent to read the letter
   B. the letter to be opened and taken care of by someone else in the organization of
   the person for whose attention it is marked is away
   C. a reply only from the specific individual
   D. to improve the appearance and balance of the letter in cases where the company
   address is a long one

50. Which one of the following would be an ACCEPTABLE way to end a business letter?   50._____

   A. Hoping you will find this information useful, I remain
   B. Yours for continuing service
   C. I hope this letter gives you the information you need
   D. Trusting this gives you the information you desire, I am

———

KEY (CORRECT ANSWERS)

1.	A	11.	B	21.	C	31.	C	41.	A
2.	D	12.	D	22.	D	32.	A	42.	A
3.	A	13.	C	23.	B	33.	D	43.	D
4.	B	14.	B	24.	D	34.	C	44.	A
5.	C	15.	B	25.	A	35.	D	45.	A
6.	B	16.	C	26.	B	36.	B	46.	D
7.	D	17.	D	27.	C	37.	A	47.	B
8.	C	18.	A	28.	D	38.	C	48.	C
9.	A	19.	C	29.	B	39.	C	49.	B
10.	A	20.	B	30.	C	40.	B	50.	C

———

TEST 2

DIRECTIONS: Each question or incomplete statement is followed by several suggested answers or completions. Select the one that BEST answers the question or completes the statement. *PRINT THE LETTER OF THE CORRECT ANSWER IN THE SPACE AT THE RIGHT.*

1. You are replying to a letter from an individual who asks for a pamphlet put out by your agency. The pamphlet is out of print. A new pamphlet with a different title, but dealing with the same subject, is available.
    Of the following, it would be BEST that your reply indicate that

    A.   you cannot send him the pamphlet he requested because it is out of print
    B.   the pamphlet he requested is out of print, but he may be able to find it in the public library
    C.   the pamphlet he requested is out of print, but you are sending him a copy of your agency's new pamphlet on the same subject
    D.   since the pamphlet he requested is out of print, you would advise him to ask his friends or business acquaintances if they have a copy of it

1.____

2. An angry citizen sends a letter to your agency claiming that your office sent him the wrong form and complaining about the general inefficiency of city workers. Upon check-ing, you find that an incorrect form was indeed sent to this person.
    In reply, you should

    A.   admit the error, apologize briefly, and enclose the correct form
    B.   send the citizen the correct form with a transmittal letter stating only that the form is enclosed
    C.   send him the correct form without any comment
    D.   advise the citizen that mistakes happen in every large organization and that you are enclosing the correct form

2.____

3. It has been suggested that the language level of a letter of reply written by a government employee be geared no higher than the probable educational level of the person to whom the letter is written.
    This suggestion is a

    A.   *good* one because it is easier for anyone to write letters simply, and this will make for a better reply
    B.   *poor* one because it is not possible to judge, from one letter, the exact educational level of the writer
    C.   *good* one because it will contribute to the recipient's comprehension of the con-tents of the letter
    D.   *poor* one because the language should be at the simplest possible level so that anyone who reads the letter can understand it

3.____

4. Suppose that a large bureau has 187 employees. On a particular day, approximately 14% of these employees are not available for work because of absences due to vacation, illness, or other reasons. Of the remaining employees, 1/7 are assigned to a special project while the balance are assigned to the normal work of the bureau.
    The number of employees assigned to the normal work of the bureau on that day is

    A.   112   B.   124   C.   138   D.   142

4.____

5. Suppose that you are in charge of a typing pool of 8 typists. Two typists type at the rate of 38 words per minute; three type at the rate of 40 words per minute; three type at the rate of 42 words per minute. The average typewritten page consists of 50 lines, 12 words per line. Each employee works from 9 to 5 with one hour off for lunch.
   The total number of pages typed by this pool in one day is, on the average, CLOSEST to _____ pages.

    A. 205   B. 225   C. 250   D. 275

  5.____

6. Suppose that part-time workers are paid $14.40 an hour, prorated to the nearest half hour, with pay guaranteed for a minimum of four hours if services are required for less than four hours. In one operation, part-time workers signed the time sheet as follows:

Worker	In	Out
A	8:00 A.M.	11:35 A.M.
B	8:30 A.M.	3:20 P.M.
C	7:55 A.M.	11:00 A.M.
D	8:30 A.M.	2:25 P.M.

How much would total payment to these part-time workers amount to tor this operation, assuming that those who stayed after 12 Noon were not paid for one hour which they took off for lunch?

    A. $268.80   B. $273.60   C. $284.40   D. $297.60

  6.____

7. He wanted to *ascertain* the facts before arriving at a conclusion.
   The word *ascertain* means MOST NEARLY

    A. disprove   B. determine   C. convert   D. provide

  7.____

8. Did the supervisor *assent* to her request for annual leave? The word *assent* means MOST NEARLY

    A. allude   B. protest   C. agree   D. refer

  8.____

9. The new worker was fearful that the others would *rebuff* her.
   The word *rebuff* means MOST NEARLY

    A. ignore   B. forget   C. copy   D. snub

  9.____

10. The supervisor of that office does not *condone* lateness. The word *condone* means MOST NEARLY

    A. mind   B. excuse   C. punish   D. remember

  10.____

11. Each employee was instructed to be as *concise* as possible when preparing a report.
    The word *concise* means MOST NEARLY

    A. exact   B. sincere   C. flexible   D. brief

  11.____

Questions 12-21.

DIRECTIONS: Below are 10 sentences numbered 12 to 21. Some of the sentences contain an error in spelling, word usage, or sentence structure, or punctuation. Some sentences are correct as they stand, although there may be other correct ways of expressing the same thought. All incorrect sentences contain only one error. Mark your answer to each question as follows:

A. if the sentence has an error in spelling
B. if the sentence has an error in punctuation or capitalization
C. if the sentence has an error in word usage or sentence structure
D. if the sentence is correct

12. Because the chairman failed to keep the participants from wandering off into irrelevant discussions, it was impossible to reach a consensus before the meeting was adjourned.   12.____

13. Certain employers have an unwritten rule that any applicant, who is over 55 years of age, is automatically excluded from consideration for any position whatsoever.   13.____

14. If the proposal to build schools in some new apartment buildings were to be accepted by the builders, one of the advantages that could be expected to result would be better communication between teachers and parents of schoolchildren.   14.____

15. In this instance, the manufacturer's violation of the law against deseptive packaging was discernible only to an experienced inspector.   15.____

16. The tenants' anger stemmed from the president's going to Washington to testify without consulting them first.   16.____

17. Did the president of this eminent banking company say; "We intend to hire and train a number of these disad-vantaged youths?"   17.____

18. In addition, today's confidential secretary must be knowledgable in many different areas: for example, she must know modern techniques for making travel arrangements for the executive.   18.____

19. To avoid further disruption of work in the offices, the protesters were forbidden from entering the building unless they had special passes.   19.____

20. A valuable secondary result of our training conferences is the opportunities afforded for management to observe the reactions of the participants.   20.____

21. Of the two proposals submitted by the committee, the first one is the best.   21.____

Questions 22-26.

DIRECTIONS: In Questions 22 through 26, choose the sentence which is BEST from the point of view of English usage suitable for a business letter or report.

22. A. It is the opinion of the Commissioners that programs which include the construction of cut-rate municipal garages in the central business district is inadvisable.   22.____
    B. Having reviewed the material submitted, the program for putting up cut-rate garages in the central business district seemed likely to cause traffic congestion.
    C. The Commissioners believe that putting up cut-rate municipal garages in the central business district is inadvisable.
    D. Making an effort to facilitate the cleaning of streets in the central business district, the building of cut-rate municipal garages presents the problem that it would encourage more motorists to come into the central city.

23. A. This letter, together with the reports, are to be sent to the principal.   23._____
       B. The reports, together with this letter, is to be sent to the principal.
       C. The reports and this letter is to be sent to the principal.
       D. This letter, together with the reports, is to be sent to the principal.

24. A. Each employee has to decide for themselves whether to take the examination.   24._____
       B. Each of the employees has to decide for himself whether to take the examination.
       C. Each of the employees has to decide for themselves whether to take the examination.
       D. Each of the employees have to decide for himself whether to take the examination.

25. A. The reason a new schedule is being prepared is that there has been a change in priorities.   25._____
       B. Because there has been a change in priorities is the reason why a new schedule is being made up.
       C. The reason why a new schedule is being made up is because there has been a change in priorities.
       D. Because of a change in priorities is the reason why a new schedule is being prepared.

26. A. The changes in procedure had an unfavorable affect upon the output of the unit.   26._____
       B. The increased output of the unit was largely due to the affect of the procedural changes.
       C. The changes in procedure had the effect of increasing the output of the unit.
       D. The increased output of the unit from the procedural changes were the effect.

Questions 27-33.

DIRECTIONS: Questions 27 through 33 are to be answered SOLELY on the basis of the information in the following extract, which is from a report prepared for Department X, which outlines the procedure to be followed in the case of transfers of employees.

Every transfer, regardless of the reason therefor, requires completion of the record of transfer, Form DT 411. To denote consent to the transfer, DT 411 should contain the signatures of the transferee and the personnel officer(s) concerned, except that, in the case of an involuntary transfer, the signatures of the transferee's present and prospective supervisors shall be entered in Boxes 8A and 8B, respectively, since the transferee does not consent. Only a permanent employee may request a transfer; in such cases, the employee's attendance record shall be duly considered with regard to absences, latenesses, and accrued overtime balances. In the case of an inter-district transfer, the employee's attendance record must be included in Section 8A of the transfer request, Form DT 410, by the personnel officer of the district from which the transfer is requested. The personnel officer of the district to which the employee requested transfer may refuse to accept accrued overtime balances in excess of ten days.

An employee on probation shall be eligible for transfer. If such employee is involuntarily transferred, he shall be credited for the period of time already served on probation. However, if such transfer is voluntary, the employee shall be required to serve the entire period of his probation in the new position. An employee who has occurred a disability which prevents him from performing his normal duties may be transferred during the period of such disability to other appropriate duties. A disability transfer requires the completion of either Form DT414 if the disability is job-connected, or Form DT 415 if it is not a job-connected disability. In either case, the personnel officer of the district from which the transfer is made signs in Box 6A of the first two copies and the personnel officer of the district to which the transfer is made signs in Box 6B of the last two copies; or, in the case of an intra-district disability transfer, the personnel officer must sign in Box 6A of the first two copies and Box 6B of the last two copies

27. When a personnel officer consents to an employee's request for transfer from his district, this procedure requires that the personnel officer sign Form(s)

    A. DT 411
    B. DT 410 and DT 411
    C. DT 411 and either Form DT 414 or DT 415
    D. DT 410 and DT 411, and either Form DT 414 or DT 415

27.____

28. With respect to the time record of an employee transferred against his wishes during his probationary period, this procedure requires that

    A. he serve the entire period of his probation in his present office
    B. he lose his accrued overtime balance
    C. his attendance record be considered with regard to absences and latenesses
    D. he be given credit for the period of time he has already served on probation

28.____

29. Assume you are a supervisor and an employee must be transferred into your office against his wishes.
According to this procedure, the box you must sign on the record of transfer is

    A. 6A   B. 8A   C. 6B   D. 8B

29.____

30. Under this procedure, in the case of a disability transfer, when must Box 6A on Forms DT 414 and DT 415 be signed by the personnel officer of the district to which the transfer is being made?

    A. In all cases when either Form DT 414 or Form DT 415 is used
    B. In all cases when Form DT 414 is used and only under certain circumstances when Form DT 415 is used
    C. In all cases when Form DT 415 is used and only under certain circumstances when Form DT 414 is used
    D. Only under certain circumstances when either Form DT 414 or Form DT 415 is used

30.____

31. From the above passage, it may be inferred MOST correctly that the number of copies of Form DT 414 is

    A. no more than 2
    B. at least 3
    C. at least 5
    D. more than the number of copies of Form DT 415

31.____

32. A change in punctuation and capitalization only which would change one sentence into two and possibly contribute to somewhat greater ease of reading of this report extract would be MOST appropriate in the _____ sentence, _____ paragraph. 32.____

   A. 2nd; 1st
   B. 3rd; 1st
   C. next to the last; 2nd
   D. 2nd; 2nd

33. In the second paragraph, a word that is INCORRECTLY used is _____ in the _____ sentence. 33.____

   A. *shall;* 1st
   B. *voluntary;* 3rd
   C. *occurred;* 4th
   D. *intra-district;* last

Questions 34-38.

DIRECTIONS: Questions 34 through 38 are to be answered SOLELY on the basis of the information contained in the following passage.

Positive discipline minimizes the amount of personal supervision required and aids in the maintenance of standards. When a new employee has been properly introduced and carefully instructed, when he has come to know the supervisor and has confidence in the supervisor's ability to take care of him, when he willingly cooperates with the supervisor, that employee has been under positive discipline and can be put on his own to produce the quantity and quality of work desired. Negative discipline, the fear of transfer to a less desirable location, for example, to a limited extent may restrain certain individuals from overt violation of rules and regulations governing attendance and conduct which in governmental agencies are usually on at least an agency-wide basis. Negative discipline may prompt employees to perform according to certain rules to avoid a penalty such as, for example, docking for tardiness.

34. According to the above passage, it is reasonable to assume that in the area of discipline, the first-line supervisor in a governmental agency has GREATER scope for action in 34.____

   A. *positive* discipline because negative discipline is largely taken care of by agency rules and regulations
   B. *negative* discipline because rules and procedures are already fixed and the supervisor can rely on them
   C. *positive* discipline because the supervisor is in a position to recommend transfers
   D. *negative* discipline because positive discipline is reserved for people on a higher supervisory level

35. In order to maintain positive discipline of employees under his supervision, it is MOST important for a supervisor to 35.____

   A. assure each employee that he has nothing to worry about
   B. insist at the outset on complete cooperation from employees
   C. be sure that each employee is well trained in his job
   D. inform new employees of the penalties for not meeting standards

36. According to the above passage, a feature of negative discipline is that it 36.____

   A. may lower employee morale
   B. may restrain employees from disobeying the rules
   C. censures equal treatment of employees
   D. tends to create standards for quality of work

37. A REASONABLE conclusion based on the above passage is that positive discipline benefits a supervisor because   37.____

    A. he can turn over orientation and supervision of a new employee to one of his subordinates
    B. subordinates learn to cooperate with one another when working on an assignment
    C. it is easier to administer
    D. it cuts down, in the long run, on the amount of time the supervisor needs to spend on direct supervision

38. Based on the above passage, it is REASONABLE to assume that an important difference between positive discipline and negative discipline is that positive discipline   38.____

    A. is concerned with the quality of work and negative discipline with the quantity of work
    B. leads to a more desirable basis for motivation of the employee
    C. is more likely to be concerned with agency rules and regulations
    D. uses fear while negative discipline uses penalties to prod employees to adequate performance

Questions 39-50.

DIRECTIONS: Questions 39 through 50 are to be answered on the basis of the information given in the graph and chart below.

ENROLLMENT IN POSTGRADUATE STUDIES

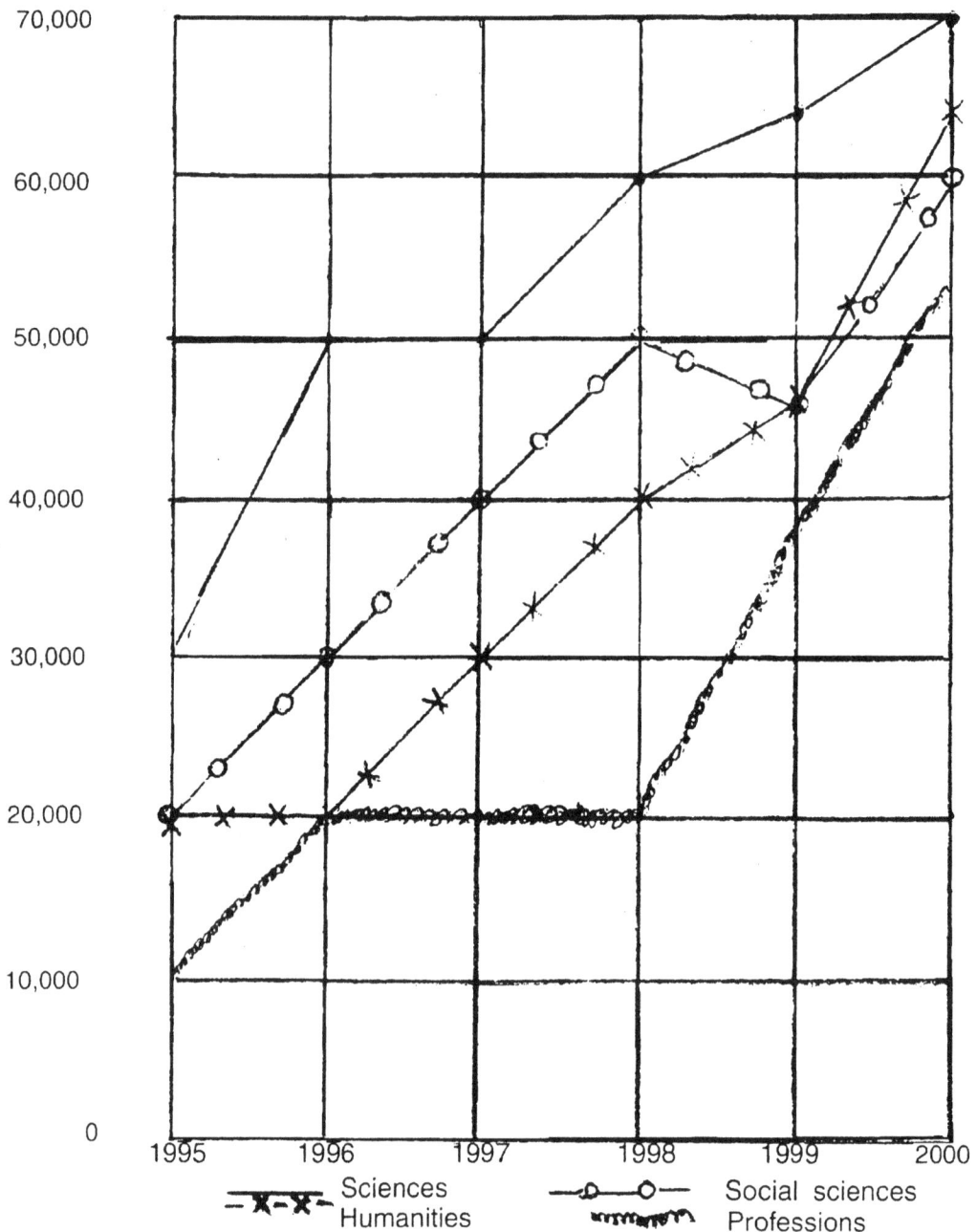

ENROLLMENT IN POSTGRADUATE STUDIES

Fields	Subdivisions	1999	2000
Sciences	Math	10,000	12,000
	Physical science	22,000	24,000
	Behavioral science	32,000	35,000
Humanities	Literature	26,000	34,000
	Philosophy	6,000	8,000
	Religion	4,000	6,000
	Arts	10,000	16,000
Social sciences	History	36,000	46,000
	Sociology	8,000	14.000
Professions	Law	2,000	2,000
	Medicine	6,000	8,000
	Business	30,000	44,000

39. The number of students enrolled in the social sciences and in the humanities was the same in _____ and _____.   39.____

     A.   1997; 1999   B.   1995; 1999
     C.   1999; 2000   D.   1996; 1999

40. A comparison of the enrollment of students in the various postgraduate studies shows that in every year from 1995 through 2000, there were more students enrolled in the _____ than in the _____.   40.____

     A.   professions; sciences
     B.   humanities; professions
     C.   social sciences; professions
     D.   humanities; sciences

41. The number of students enrolled in the humanities was GREATER than the number of students enrolled in the professions by the same amount in _____ of the years.   41.____

     A.   two   B.   three   C.   four   D.   five

42. The one field of postgraduate study to show a decrease in enrollment in one year compared to the year immediately preceding is   42.____

     A.   humanities   B.   sciences
     C.   professions   D.   social sciences

43. If the proportion of arts students to all humanities students was the same in 1997 as in 2000, then the number of arts students in 1997 was   43.____

     A.   7,500   B.   13,000   C.   15,000   D.   5,000

44. In which field of postgraduate study did enrollment INCREASE by 20 percent from 1997 to 1998?   44.____

     A.   Humanities   B.   Professions
     C.   Sciences   D.   Social sciences

45. The GREATEST increase in overall enrollment took place between   45.____

     A.   1995 and 1996   B.   1997 and 1998
     C.   1998 and 1999   D.   1999 and 2000

46. Between 1997 and 2000, the combined enrollment of the sciences and social sciences increased by   46.____

    A. 40,000   B. 48,000   C. 50,000   D. 54,000

47. If the enrollment in the social sciences had decreased from 1999 to 2000 at the same rate as from 1998 to 1999, then the social science enrollment in 2000 would have differed from the humanities enrollment in 2000 *MOST* NEARLY by   47.____

    A. 6,000   B. 8,000   C. 12,000   D. 22,000

48. In the humanities, the GREATEST percentage increase in enrollment from 1999 to 2000 was in   48.____

    A. literature   B. philosophy
    C. religion   D. arts

49. If the proportion of behavioral science students to the total number of students in the sciences was the same in 1996 as in 1999, then the increase in behavioral science enrollment from 1996 to 2000 was   49.____

    A. 5,000   B. 7,000   C. 10,000   D. 14,000

50. If enrollment in the professions increased at the same rate from 2000 to 2001 as from 1999 to 2000, the enrollment in the professions in 2001 would be MOST NEARLY   50.____

    A. 85,000   B. 75,000   C. 60,000   D. 55,000

KEY (CORRECT ANSWERS)

1. C	11. D	21. C	31. B	41. B
2. A	12. C	22. C	32. B	42. D
3. C	13. B	23. D	33. C	43. A
4. C	14. D	24. B	34. A	44. C
5. B	15. A	25. A	35. C	45. D
6. B	16. D	26. C	36. B	46. A
7. B	17. B	27. A	37. D	47. D
8. C	18. A	28. D	38. B	48. D
9. D	19. C	29. D	39. B	49. C
10. B	20. D	30. D	40. C	50. B

EXAMINATION SECTION
TEST 1

DIRECTIONS: Each question or incomplete statement is followed by several suggested answers or completions. Select the one that BEST answers the question or completes the statement. *PRINT THE LETTER OF THE CORRECT ANSWER IN THE SPACE AT THE RIGHT.*

Questions 1-4.

DIRECTIONS: Answer Questions 1 through 4 SOLELY on the basis of the following passage.

Job analysis combined with performance appraisal is an excellent method of determining training needs of individuals. The steps in this method are to determine the specific duties of the job, to evaluate the adequacy with which the employee performs each of these duties, and finally to determine what significant improvements can be made by training.

The list of duties can be obtained in a number of ways: asking the employee, asking the supervisor, observing the employee, etc. Adequacy of performance can be estimated by the employee, but the supervisor's evaluation must also be obtained. This evaluation will usually be based on observation.

What does the supervisor observe? The employee, while he is working; the employee's work relationships; the ease, speed, and sureness of the employee's actions; the way he applies himself to the job; the accuracy and amount of completed work; its conformity with established procedures and standards; the appearance of the work; the soundness of judgment it shows; and, finally, signs of good or poor communication, understanding, and cooperation among employees.

Such observation is a normal and inseparable part of the everyday job of supervision. Systematically, recorded, evaluated, and summarized, it highlights both general and individual training needs.

1. According to the passage, job analysis may be used by the supervisor in   1.____

    A. increasing his own understanding of tasks performed in his unit
    B. increasing efficiency of communication within the organization
    C. assisting personnel experts in the classification of positions
    D. determining in which areas an employee needs more instruction

2. According to the passage, the FIRST step in determining the training needs of employ-   2.____
ees is to

    A. locate the significant improvements that can be made by training
    B. determine the specific duties required in a job
    C. evaluate the employee's performance
    D. motivate the employee to want to improve himself

3. On the basis of the above passage, which of the following is the BEST way for a supervi-   3.____
sor to determine the adequacy of employee performance?

    A. Check the accuracy and amount of completed work
    B. Ask the training officer
    C. Observe all aspects of the employee's work
    D. Obtain the employee's own estimate

4. Which of the following is NOT mentioned by the passage as a factor to be taken into consideration in judging the adequacy of employee performance?

    A. Accuracy of completed work
    B. Appearance of completed work
    C. Cooperation among employees
    D. Attitude of the employee toward his supervisor

4.____

5. In indexing names of business firms and other organizations, ONE of the rules to be followed is:

    A. The word *and* is considered an indexing unit
    B. When a firm name includes the full name of a person who is not well-known, the person's first name is considered as the first indexing unit
    C. Usually the units in a firm name are indexed in the order in which they are written
    D. When a firm's name is made up of single letters (such as ABC Corp.), the letters taken together are considered more than one indexing unit

5.____

6. Assume that people often come to your office with complaints of errors in your agency's handling of their clients. The employees in your office have the job of listening to these complaints and investigating them. One day, when it is almost closing time, a person comes into your office, apparently very angry, and demands that you take care of his complaint at once.
Your IMMEDIATE reaction should be to

    A. suggest that he return the following day
    B. find out his name and the nature of his complaint
    C. tell him to write a letter
    D. call over your superior

6.____

7. Assume that part of your job is to notify people concerning whether their applications for a certain program have been approved or disapproved. However, you do not actually make the decision on approval or disapproval. One day, you answer a telephone call from a woman who states that she has not yet received any word on her application. She goes on to tell you her qualifications for the program. From what she has said, you know that persons with such qualifications are usually approved.
Of the following, which one is the BEST thing for you to say to her?

    A. "You probably will be accepted, but wait until you receive a letter before trying to join the program."
    B. "Since you seem well qualified, I am sure that your application will be approved."
    C. "If you can write us a letter emphasizing your qualifications, it may speed up the process."
    D. "You will be notified of the results of your application as soon as a decision has been made."

7.____

8. Suppose that one of your duties includes answering specific telephone inquiries. Your superior refers a call to you from an irate person who claims that your agency is inefficient and is wasting taxpayers' money.
Of the following, the BEST way to handle such a call is to

    A. listen briefly and then hang up without answering
    B. note the caller's comments and tell him that you will transmit them to your superiors

8.____

C. connect the caller with the head of your agency
D. discuss your own opinions with the caller

9. An employee has been assigned to open her division head's mail and place it on his   9._____
desk. One day, the employee opens a letter which she then notices is marked *Personal*.
Of the following, the BEST action for her to take is to

    A. write *Personal* on the letter and staple the envelope to the back of the letter
    B. ignore the matter and treat the letter the same way as the others
    C. give it to another division head to hold until her own division head comes into the
       office
    D. leave the letter in the envelope and write *Sorry opened by mistake* on the envelope
       and initial it

Questions 10-14.

DIRECTIONS: Questions 10 through 14 each consist of a quotation which contains one word
that is incorrectly used because it is not in keeping with the meaning that the
quotation is evidently intended to convey. Of the words underlined in each quotation, determine which word is incorrectly used. Then select from among the
words lettered A, B, C, and D the word which, when substituted for the incorrectly used word, would BEST help to convey the meaning of the quotation.
(Do NOT indicate a change for an underlined word unless the underlined word
is incorrectly used.)

10. Unless reasonable managerial supervision is <u>exercised</u> over office supplies, it is certain   10._____
that there will be extravagance, <u>rejected</u> items out of stock, <u>excessive</u> prices paid for certain items, and <u>obsolete</u> material in the stockroom.

    A. overlooked   B. immoderate
    C. needed   D. instituted

11. Since <u>office</u> supplies are in such <u>common</u> use, an attitude of indifference about their han-   11._____
dling is not <u>unusual</u>. Their importance is often recognized only when they are <u>utilized</u> or
out of stock, for office employees must have proper supplies if maximum productivity is to
be <u>attained</u>.

    A. plentiful   B. unavailable
    C. reduced   D. expected

12. Anyone <u>effected</u> by paperwork, <u>interested</u> in or engaged in office work, or desiring to   12._____
improve <u>informational</u> activities can find materials <u>keyed</u> to his needs.

    A. attentive   B. available   C. affected   D. ambitious

13. Information is <u>homogeneous</u> and must therefore be properly classified so that each type   13._____
may be <u>employed</u> in ways <u>appropriate</u> to its <u>own peculiar</u> properties.

    A. apparent   B. heterogeneous
    C. consistent   D. idiosyncratic

14. <u>Intellectual</u> training may seem a <u>formidable</u> phrase, but it means nothing more than the   14._____
<u>deliberate</u> cultivation of the ability to think, and there is no <u>dark</u> contrast between the
intellectual and the practical.

A.   subjective   B.   objective
C.   sharp   D.   vocational

15.   The MOST important reason for having a filing system is to   15._____

     A.   get papers out of the way
     B.   have a record of everything that has happened
     C.   retain information to justify your actions
     D.   enable rapid retrieval of information

16.   The system of filing which is used MOST frequently is called _____ filing.   16._____

     A.   alphabetic   B.   alphanumeric
     C.   geographic   D.   numeric

17.   One of the clerks under your supervision has been telephoning frequently to tell you that   17._____
he was taking the day off. Unless there is a real need for it, taking leave which is not
scheduled is frowned upon because it upsets the work schedule.
Under these circumstances, which of the following reasons for taking the day off is
MOST acceptable?

     A.   "I can't work when my arthritis bothers me."
     B.   "I've been pressured with work from my night job and needed the extra time to
        catch up."
     C.   "My family just moved to a new house, and I needed the time to start the repairs."
     D.   "Work here has not been challenging, and I've been looking for another job."

18.   One of the employees under your supervision, previously a very satisfactory worker, has   18._____
begun arriving late one or two mornings each week. No explanation has been offered for
this change. You call her to your office for a conference. As you are explaining the purpose of the conference and your need to understand this sudden lateness problem, she
becomes angry and states that you have no right to question her.
Of the following, the BEST course of action for you to take at this point is to

     A.   inform her in your most authoritarian tone that you are the supervisor and that you
        have every right to question her
     B.   end the conference and advise the employee that you will have no further discus-
        sion with her until she controls her temper
     C.   remain calm, try to calm her down, and when she has quieted, explain the reasons
        for your questions and the need for answers
     D.   hold your temper; when she has calmed down, tell her that you will not have a
        tardy worker in your unit and will have her transferred at once

19.   Assume that, in the branch of the agency for which you work, you are the only clerical   19._____
person on the staff with a supervisory title and, in addition, that you are the office manager. On a particular day when all members of the professional staff are away from the
building attending an important meeting, an urgent call comes through requesting some
confidential information ordinarily released only by professional staff.
Of the following, the MOST reasonable action for you to take is to

     A.   decline to give the information because you are not a member of the professional
        staff
     B.   offer to call back after you get permission from the agency director at the main
        office

C. advise the caller that you will supply the information as soon as your chief returns
D. supply the information requested and inform your chief when she returns

20. As a supervisor, you are scheduled to attend an important conference with your superior.   20.____
However, that day you learn that your very capable assistant is ill and unable to come to
work. Several highly sensitive tasks are scheduled for completion on this day.
Of the following, the BEST way to handle this situation is to

A. tell your supervisor you cannot attend the meeting and ask that it be postponed
B. assign one of your staff to see that the jobs are completed and turned in
C. advise your supervisor of the situation and ask what you should do
D. call the departments for which the work is being done and ask for an extension of
time

21. When a decision needs to be made which is likely to affect units other than his own, a   21.____
supervisor should USUALLY

A. make such a decision quickly and then discuss it with his supervisor
B. make such a decision only after careful consultation with his subordinates
C. discuss the problem with his immediate superior before making such a decision
D. have his subordinates arrive at such a decision in conference with the subordi-
nates in the other units

22. Assume that, as a supervisor in Division X, you are training Ms. Y, a new employee, to   22.____
answer the telephone properly.
You should explain that the BEST way to answer is to pick up the receiver and say:

A. "What is your name, please?"
B. "May I help you?"
C. "Ms. Y speaking."
D. "Division X, Ms. Y speaking."

Questions 23-25.

DIRECTIONS: Questions 23 through 25 consist of sentences in which two words are missing.
Examine each sentence, and then choose from below it the words which
should be inserted in the blank spaces in order to create a coherent and well-
written sentence.

23. Human behavior is far _____ variable, and therefore _____ predictable, than that of   23.____
any other species.

A. less; as   B. less; not
C. more; not   D. more; less

24. The _____ limitation of this method is that the results are based _____ a narrow sam-   24.____
ple.

A. chief; with   B. chief; on
C. only; for   D. only; to

25. Although there _____ a standard procedure for handling these problems, each case   25.____
often has _____ own unique features.

A. are; its   B. are; their
C. is; its   D. is; their

KEY (CORRECT ANSWERS)

1.	D		11.	B
2.	B		12.	C
3.	C		13.	B
4.	D		14.	C
5.	C		15.	D
6.	B		16.	A
7.	D		17.	A
8.	B		18.	C
9.	D		19.	B
10.	C		20.	C

21. C
22. D
23. D
24. B
25. C

TEST 2

DIRECTIONS: Each question or incomplete statement is followed by several suggested answers or completions. Select the one that BEST answers your question or completes the statement. *PRINT THE LETTER OF THE CORRECT ANSWER IN THE SPACE AT THE RIGHT.*

Questions 1-3.

DIRECTIONS: Questions 1 through 3 each consist of a group of four sentences. Read each sentence carefully, and select the one of the four in each group which represents the BEST English usage for business letters and reports.

1. A. The chairman himself, rather than his aides, hasreviewed the report.   1._____
    B. The chairman himself, rather than his aides, have reviewed the report.
    C. The chairmen, not the aide, has reviewed the report.
    D. The aide, not the chairmen, have reviewed the report.

2. A. Various proposals were submitted but the decision is not been made.   2._____
    B. Various proposals has been submitted but the decision has not been made.
    C. Various proposals were submitted but the decision is not been made.
    D. Various proposals have been submitted but the decision has not been made.

3. A. Everyone were rewarded for his successful attempt.   3._____
    B. They were successful in their attempts and each of them was rewarded.
    C. Each of them are rewarded for their successful attempts.
    D. The reward for their successful attempts were made to each of them.

4. Which of the following is MOST suited to arrangement in chronological order?   4._____

    A. Applications for various types and levels of jobs
    B. Issues of a weekly publication
    C. Weekly time cards for all employees for the week of April 21
    D. Personnel records for all employees

5. Words that are *synonymous* with a given word ALWAYS   5._____

    A. have the same meaning as the given word
    B. have the same pronunciation as the given word
    C. have the opposite meaning of the given word
    D. can be rhymed with the given word

Questions 6-11.

DIRECTIONS: Answer Questions 6 through 11 on the basis of the following chart showing numbers of errors made by four clerks in one work unit for a half-year period.

	Allan	Barry	Cary	David
July	5	4	1	7
Aug.	8	3	9	8
Sept.	7	8	7	5
Oct.	3	6	5	3
Nov.	2	4	4	6
Dec.	5	2	8	4

6. The clerk with the HIGHEST number of errors for the six-month period was   6.____

   A. Allan   B. Barry   C. Cary   D. David

7. If the number of errors made by Allan in the six months shown represented one-eighth of   7.____
the total errors made by the unit during the entire year, what was the TOTAL number of
errors made by the unit for the year?

   A. 124   B. 180   C. 240   D. 360

8. The number of errors made by David in November was what FRACTION of the total   8.____
errors made in November?

   A. 1/3   B. 1/6   C. 3/8   D. 3/16

9. The average number of errors made per month per clerk was MOST NEARLY   9.____

   A. 4   B. 5   C. 6   D. 7

10. Of the total number of errors made during the six-month period, the percentage made in   10.____
August was MOST NEARLY

   A. 2%   B. 4%   C. 23%   D. 44%

11. If the number of errors in the unit were to decrease in the next six months by 30%, what   11.____
would be MOST NEARLY the total number of errors for the unit for the next six months?

   A. 87   B. 94   C. 120   D. 137

12. The arithmetic mean salary for five employees earning $18,500, $18,300, $18,600,   12.____
$18,400, and $18,500, respectively, is

   A. $18,450   B. $18,460   C. $18,475   D. $18,500

13. Last year, a city department which is responsible for purchasing supplies ordered bond   13.____
paper in equal quantities from 22 different companies. The price was exactly the same
for each company, and the total cost for the 22 orders was $693,113.
Assuming prices did not change during the year, the cost of EACH order was MOST
NEARLY

   A. $31,490   B. $31,495   C. $31,500   D. $31,505

14. A city agency engaged in repair work uses a small part which the city purchases for 14?   14.____
each. Assume that, in a certain year, the total expenditure of the city for this part was
$700.
How MANY of these parts were purchased that year?

   A. 50   B. 200   C. 2,000   D. 5,000

15. The work unit which you supervise is responsible for processing fifteen reports per month.
    If your unit has four clerks and the best worker completes 40% of the reports himself, how many reports would each of the other clerks have to complete if they all do an equal number?

    A. 1   B. 2   C. 3   D. 4

    15.____

16. Assume that the work unit in which you work has 24 clerks and 18 stenographers.
    In order to change the ratio of stenographers to clerks so that there is one stenographer for every four clerks, it would be necessary to REDUCE the number of stenographers by

    A. 3   B. 6   C. 9   D. 12

    16.____

17. Assume that your office is responsible for opening and distributing all the mail of the division. After opening a letter, one of your subordinates notices that it states that there should be an enclosure in the envelope. However, there is no enclosure in the envelope. Of the following, the BEST instruction that you can give the clerk is to

    A. call the sender to obtain the enclosure
    B. call the addressee to inform him that the enclosure is missing
    C. note the omission in the margin of the letter
    D. forward the letter without taking any action

    17.____

18. While opening the envelope containing official correspondence, you accidentally cut the enclosed letter.
    Of the following, the BEST action for you to take is to

    A. leave the material as it is
    B. put it together by using transparent mending tape
    C. keep it together by putting it back in the envelope
    D. keep it together by using paper clips

    18.____

19. Suppose your supervisor is on the telephone in his office and an applicant arrives for a scheduled interview with him.
    Of the following, the BEST procedure to follow ordinarily is to

    A. informally chat with the applicant in your office until your supervisor has finished his phone conversation
    B. escort him directly into your supervisor's office and have him wait for him there
    C. inform your supervisor of the applicant's arrival and try to make the applicant feel comfortable while waiting
    D. have him hang up his coat and tell him to go directly in to see your supervisor

    19.____

20. The length of time that files should be kept is GENERALLY

    A. considered to be seven years
    B. dependent upon how much new material has accumulated in the files
    C. directly proportionate to the number of years the office has been in operation
    D. dependent upon the type and nature of the material in the files

    20.____

21. Cross-referencing a document when you file it means 21.____
    A. making a copy of the document and putting the copy into a related file
    B. indicating on the front of the document the name of the person who wrote it, the date it was written, and for what purpose
    C. putting a special sheet or card in a related file to indicate where the document is filed
    D. indicating on the document where it is to be filed

22. Unnecessary handling and recording of incoming mail could be eliminated by 22.____
    A. having the person who opens it initial it
    B. indicating on the piece of mail the names of all the individuals who should see it
    C. sending all incoming mail to more than one central location
    D. making a photocopy of each piece of incoming mail

23. Of the following, the office tasks which lend themselves MOST readily to planning and study are 23.____
    A. repetitive, occur in volume, and extend over a period of time
    B. cyclical in nature, have small volume, and extend over a short period of time
    C. tasks which occur only once in a great while not according to any schedule, and have large volume
    D. special tasks which occur only once, regardless of their volume and length of time

24. A good recordkeeping system includes all of the following procedures EXCEPT the 24.____
    A. filing of useless records
    B. destruction of certain files
    C. transferring of records from one type of file to another
    D. creation of inactive files

25. Assume that, as a supervisor, you are responsible for orienting and training new employ- 25.____
    ees in your unit. Which of the following can MOST properly be omitted from your discussions with a new employee?
    A. The purpose of commonly used office forms
    B. Time and leave regulations
    C. Procedures for required handling of routine business calls
    D. The reason the last employee was fired

KEY (CORRECT ANSWERS)

1.	A		11.	A
2.	D		12.	B
3.	B		13.	D
4.	B		14.	D
5.	A		15.	C
6.	C		16.	D
7.	C		17.	C
8.	C		18.	B
9.	B		19.	C
10.	C		20.	D

21.	C
22.	B
23.	A
24.	A
25.	D

EXAMINATION SECTION
TEST 1

DIRECTIONS: Each question or incomplete statement is followed by several suggested answers or completions. Select the one that BEST answers the question or completes the statement. *PRINT THE LETTER OF THE CORRECT ANSWER IN THE SPACE AT THE RIGHT.*

1.   A certain system for handling office supplies requires that supplies be issued to the various agency offices only on a bi-weekly basis and that all supply requisitions be authorized by the unit supervisor.
The BEST reason for establishing this supplies system is to

    A.   standardize ordering descriptions and stock identification codes
    B.   prevent the disordering of stock shelves and cabinets by unauthorized persons searching for supplies
    C.   ensure that unit supervisors properly exercise their right to make determinations on supply orders
    D.   encourage proper utilization of supplies to control the workload

1.____

2.   It is important that every office have a retention and disposal program for filing material. Suppose that you have been appointed administrative assistant in an office with a poorly organized records-retention program.
In establishing a revised program for the transfer or disposal of records, the step which would logically be taken THIRD in the process is

    A.   preparing a safe and inexpensive storage area and setting up an indexing system for records already in storage
    B.   determining what papers to retain and for how long a period
    C.   taking an inventory of what is filed, where it is filed, how much is filed, and how often it is used
    D.   moving records from active to inactive files and destroying useless records

2.____

3.   In the effective design of office forms, the FIRST step to take is to

    A.   decide what information should be included
    B.   decide the purpose for which the form will be used
    C.   identify the form by name and number
    D.   identify the employees who will be using the form

3.____

4.   Some designers of office forms prefer to locate the instructions on how to fill out the form at the bottom of it. The MOST logical objection to placing such instructions at the bottom of the form is that

    A.   instructions at the bottom require an excess of space
    B.   all form instructions should be outlined with a separate paragraph
    C.   the form may be partly filled out before the instructions are seen
    D.   the bottom of the form should be reserved only for authorization and signature

4.____

5. A formal business report may consist of many parts, including the following: 5.____
   - I. Table of contents
   - II. List of references
   - III. Preface
   - IV. Index
   - V. List of tables
   - VI. Conclusions or recommendations

   Of the following, in setting up a formal report, the PROPER order of the six parts listed
   is

   A. I, III, VI, V, II, IV   B. IV, III, II, V, VI, I
   C. III, I, V, VI, II, IV   D. II, V, III, I, IV, VI

6. Three of the basic functions of office management are considered to be planning, con- 6.____
   trolling, and organizing. Of the following, the one which might BEST be considered
   ORGANIZING activity is

   A. assigning personnel and materials to work units to achieve agreed-upon objectives
   B. determining future objectives and indicating conditions affecting the accomplish-
      ment of the goals
   C. evaluating accomplishments and applying necessary corrective measures to
      insure results
   D. motivating employees to perform their work in accordance with objectives

7. The following four statements relate to office layout. 7.____
   - I. Position supervisors' desks at the front of their work group so that they can
        easily be recognized as persons in authority
   - II. Arrange file cabinets and frequently used equipment near the employees
        who utilize them most often
   - III. Locate the receptionist's desk near the entrance of the office so that visitor
        traffic will not distract other workers
   - IV. Divide a large office area into many smaller offices by using stationary parti-
        tions so that all employees may have privacy and prestige

   According to authorities in office management and administration, which of these
   statements are GENERALLY recommended guides to effective office layout?

   A. I, II, III   B. II, III, IV
   C. II, III   D. All of the above

8. For which of the following purposes would a flow chart have the GREATEST applicabil- 8.____
   ity?

   A. Training new employees in performance of routinized duties
   B. Determining adequacy of performance of employees
   C. Determining the accuracy of the organization chart
   D. Locating causes of delays in carrying out an operation

9. Office work management concerns tangible accomplishment or production. It has to do 9.____
   with results; it does not deal with the amount of energy expended by the individual who
   produces the results.
   According to this statement, the production in which of the following kinds of jobs
   would be MOST difficult to measure accurately? A(n)

A.   file clerk
B.   secretary
C.   computer operator
D.   office administrator

10.   The FIRST step in the statistical analysis of a great mass of data secured from a survey   10.____
is to

A.   scan the data to determine which is atypical of the survey
B.   determine the number of deviations from the average
C.   arrange the data into groups on the basis of likenesses and differences
D.   plot the data on a graph to determine trends

11.   Suppose that, as an administrative assistant in charge of an office, you are required to   11.____
change the layout of your office to accommodate expanding functions.
The LEAST important factor to be considered in planning the revised layout is the

A.   relative productivity of individuals in the office
B.   communication and work flow needs
C.   need for screening confidential activities from unauthorized persons
D.   areas of noise concentration

12.   Suppose you have instructed a new employee to follow a standardized series of steps to   12.____
accomplish a job. He is to use a rubber stamp, then a red pencil on the first paper, and a
numbering machine on the second. Then, he is to staple the two sheets of paper together
and put them to one side. You observe, however, that he sometimes uses the red pencil
first, sometimes the numbering machine first. At other times, he does the stapling before
using the numbering machine.
For you as supervisor to suggest that the clerk use the standardized method when
doing this job would be

A.   *bad*, because the clerk should be given a chance to use his independent judgment
on the best way to do his job
B.   *good*, because the clerk's sequence of actions results in a loss of efficiency
C.   *bad*, because it is not wise to interrupt the work habit the clerk has already developed
D.   *good*, because the clerk should not be permitted to make unauthorized changes in
standard office routines

13.   Suppose study of the current records management system for students' transcripts   13.____
reveals needless recopying of transcript data throughout various offices within the university. On this basis, a recommendation is made that this unnecessary recopying of information be eliminated.
This decision to eliminate waste in material, time, and space is an application of the
office management principle of

A.   work simplification
B.   routing and scheduling
C.   job analysis
D.   cost and budgetary control

14.   It is generally LEAST practical for an office manager to prepare for known peak work   14.____
periods by

A.   putting job procedures into writing so that they can be handled by more than one
person
B.   arranging to make assignments of work on a short-interval scheduling basis

C.   cleaning up as much work as possible ahead of known peak periods
D.   rotating jobs and assignments among different employees to assure staff flexibility

15. The four statements below are about office manuals used for various purposes.   15.____
If you had the job of designing and controlling several kinds of office manuals to be
used in your agency, which one of these statements would BEST apply as a general
rule for you to follow?

A.   Office manual content should be classified into main topics with proper subdivisions arranged in strict alphabetical order.
B.   Manual additions and revisions should be distributed promptly to all holders of
manuals for their approval, correction, and criticism.
C.   The language used in office manuals should be simple, and charts and diagrams
should be interspersed within the narrative material for further clarity.
D.   Office manual content should be classified into main topics arranged in strict alphabetical order with subtopics in sequence according to importance.

16. Suppose that, as an administrative assistant, you have been assigned to plan the reorga- 16.____
nization of an office which has not been operating efficiently because of the uncoordi-
nated manner in which new functions have been assigned to it over the past year.
The FIRST thing you should do is

A.   call a meeting of the office staff and explain the purposes of the planned reorgani-
zation
B.   make a cost-value analysis of the present operations to determine what should be
changed or eliminated
C.   prepare a diagram of the flow of work as you think it should be
D.   define carefully the current objectives to be achieved by this reorganization

17. Effective organization requires that specific actions be taken in proper sequence.   17.____
The following are four actions essential to effective organization:
     I.   Group activities on the basis of human and material resources
     II.   Coordinate functions and provide for good communications
     III.   Formulate objectives, policies, and plans
     IV.   Determine activities necessary to accomplish goals
The PROPER sequence of these four actions is:

A. III, II, IV, I   B. IV, III, I, II
C. III, IV, I, II   D. IV, I, III, II

18. For an administrative assistant to give each of his subordinates exactly the same type of 18.____
supervision is

A.   *advisable,* because he will gain a reputation for being fair and impartial
B.   *inadvisable,* because subordinates work more diligently when they think they are
receiving preferential treatment
C.   *advisable,* because most human problems can be classified into categories which
make them easier to handle
D.   *inadvisable,* because people differ and there is no one supervisory procedure that
applies in every case to dealing with individuals

19. Suppose that, as an administrative assistant, you find that some of your subordinates are coming to you with complaints you think are trivial.
For you to hear them through is

   A. *poor practice*; subordinates should be trained to come to you only with major grievances
   B. *good practice*; major grievances sometimes are the underlying cause of minor complaints
   C. *poor practice*; you should delegate this kind of matter and spend your time on more important problems
   D. *good practice*; this will make you more popular with your subordinates

19.____

20. Suppose that a new departmental policy has just been established which you feel may be resented by your subordinates, but which they must understand and follow. Which would it be most advisable for you as their supervisor to do FIRST?

   A. Make clear to your subordinates that you are not responsible for making this policy.
   B. Tell your subordinates that you agree with the policy whether you do or not.
   C. Explain specifically to your subordinates the reasons for the policy and how it is going to affect them.
   D. Distribute a memo outlining the new policy and require your subordinates to read it.

20.____

21. An office assistant under your supervision tells you that she is reluctant to speak to one of her subordinates about poor work habits because this subordinate is strong-willed, and she does not want to antagonize her.
For you to refuse the office assistant's request that you speak to her subordinate about this matter is

   A. *inadvisable,* since you are in a position of greater authority
   B. *advisable,* since supervision of this subordinate is a basic responsibility of that office assistant
   C. *inadvisable,* since the office assistant must work more closely with her subordinate than you do
   D. *advisable,* since you should not risk antagonizing her subordinate yourself

21.____

22. The GREATEST advantage to a supervisor of using oral communications as compared to written is the

   A. opportunity provided for immediate feedback
   B. speed with which orders can be given and carried out
   C. reduction in amount of paper work
   D. establishment of an informal atmosphere

22.____

23. Of the following, the MOST important reason for an administrative assistant to have private, face-to-face discussions with subordinates about their performance is

   A. encourage a more competitive spirit among employees
   B. give special praise to employees who perform well
   C. discipline employees who perform poorly
   D. help employees improve their work

23.____

24. For a supervisor to keep records of reprimands to subordinates about violations of rules is   24._____

   A. *poor practice*; such records are evidence of the supervisor's inability to maintain discipline
   B. *good practice*; these records are valuable to support disciplinary actions recommended or taken
   C. *poor practice*; the best way to prevent recurrences is to apply penalties without delay
   D. *good practice*; such records are evidence that the supervisor is doing a good job

25. As an administrative assistant supervising a small office, you decide to hold a staff meeting to try to find an acceptable solution to a problem that is causing serious conflicts within the group.   25._____
   At this meeting, your role should be to present the problem and

   A. see that the group keeps the problem in focus and does not discuss irrelevant matters
   B. act as chairman of the meeting, but take no other part in the discussion
   C. see to it that each member of the group offers a suggestion for its solution
   D. state your views on the matter before any discussion gets under way

---

KEY (CORRECT ANSWERS)

1.	D		11.	A
2.	A		12.	B
3.	B		13.	A
4.	C		14.	B
5.	C		15.	C
6.	A		16.	D
7.	C		17.	C
8.	D		18.	D
9.	D		19.	B
10.	C		20.	C

21.	B
22.	A
23.	D
24.	B
25.	A

TEST 2

DIRECTIONS: Each question or incomplete statement is followed by several suggested answers or completions. Select the one that BEST answers the question or completes the statement. *PRINT THE LETTER OF THE CORRECT ANSWER IN THE SPACE AT THE RIGHT.*

1. Suppose that one of your subordinates who supervises two young office assistants has been late for work a number of times and you have decided to talk to him about it.
In your discussion, it would be MOST constructive for you to emphasize that   1._____

    A. personal problems cannot be used as an excuse for these latenesses
    B. the department suffers financially when he is late
    C. you will be forced to give him a less desirable assignment if his latenesses continue
    D. his latenesses set a bad example to those he supervises

2. Suppose that, as a newly-appointed administrative assistant, you are in charge of a small but very busy office. Your four subordinates are often required to make quick decisions on a wide range of matters while answering telephone or in-person inquiries.
You can MOST efficiently help your subordinates meet such situations by   2._____

    A. delegating authority to make such decisions to only one or two trusted subordinates
    B. training each subordinate in the proper response for each kind of inquiry that might be made
    C. making certain that subordinates understand clearly the basic policies that affect these decisions
    D. making each subordinate an expert in one area

3. Of the following, the MOST recent development in methods of training supervisors that involves the human relations approach is   3._____

    A. conference training   B. the lecture method
    C. the case method   D. sensitivity training

4. Which of the following is MOST likely to result in failure as a supervisor?   4._____

    A. Showing permissiveness in relations with subordinates
    B. Avoiding delegation of tasks to subordinates
    C. Setting high performance standards for subordinates
    D. Using discipline only when necessary

5. The MOST important long-range benefit to an organization of proper delegation of work by supervisors is *generally* that   5._____

    A. subordinates will be developed to assume greater responsibilities
    B. subordinates will perform the work as their supervisors would
    C. errors in delegated work will be eliminated
    D. more efficient communication among organizational components will result

6. Which of the following duties would it be LEAST appropriate for an administrative assistant in charge of an office to delegate to an immediate subordinate?

    A. Checking of figures to be used in a report to the head of the department
    B. On-the-job training of newly appointed college office assistants
    C. Reorganization of assignments for higher level office staff
    D. Contacting other school offices for needed information

6._____

7. Decisions should be delegated to the lowest point in the organization at which they can be made effectively.
The one of the following which is MOST likely to be a result of the application of this accepted management principle is that

    A. upward communications will be facilitated
    B. potential for more rapid decisions and implementation is increased
    C. coordination of decisions that are made will be simplified
    D. no important factors will be overlooked in making decisions

7._____

8. The lecture-demonstration method would be LEAST desirable in a training program set up for

    A. changing the attitudes of long-term employees
    B. informing subordinates about new procedures
    C. explaining how a new office machine works
    D. orientation of new employees

8._____

9. Which one of the following conditions would be LEAST likely to indicate a need for employee training?

    A. Large number of employee suggestions
    B. Large amount of overtime
    C. High number of chronic latenesses
    D. Low employee morale

9._____

10. An administrative assistant is planning to make a recommendation to change a procedure which would substantially affect the work of his subordinates.
For this supervisor to consult with his subordinates about the recommendation before sending it through would be

    A. *undesirable;* subordinates may lose respect for a supervisor who evidences such indecisiveness
    B. *desirable;* since the change in procedure would affect their work, subordinates should decide whether the change should be made
    C. *undesirable;* since subordinates would not receive credit if the procedure were changed, their morale would be lowered
    D. *desirable;* the subordinates may have some worthwhile suggestions concerning the recommendation

10._____

11. The BEST way to measure improvement in a selected group of office assistants who have undergone a training course in the use of specific techniques is to

    A. have the trainees fill out questionnaires at the completion of the course as to what they have learned and giving their opinions as to the value of the course

11._____

B. compare the performance of the trainees who completed the course with the performance of office assistants who did not take the course
C. compare the performance of the trainees in these techniques before and after the training course
D. compare the degree of success on the next promotion examination of trainees and non-trainees

12. When an administrative assistant finds it necessary to call in a subordinate for a disciplinary interview, his MAIN objective should be to   12._____

    A. use techniques which can penetrate any deception and get at the truth
    B. stress correction of, rather than punishment for, past errors
    C. maintain a reputation for being an understanding superior
    D. decide on disciplinary action that is consistent with penalties applied for similar infractions

13. Suppose that a newly promoted office assistant does satisfactory work during the first   13._____
five months of her probationary period. However, her supervisor notices shortly after this time that her performance is falling below acceptable standards. The supervisor decides to keep records of this employee's performance, and if there is no significant improvement by the end of 11 months, to recommend that this employee not be given tenure in the higher title.
This, as the sole course of action, is

    A. *justified;* employees who do not perform satisfactorily should not be promoted
    B. *unjustified;* the supervisor should attempt to determine the cause of the poor performance as soon as possible
    C. *justified;* the supervisor will have given the subordinate the full probationary period to improve herself
    D. *unjustified;* the subordinate should be demoted to her previous title as soon as her work becomes unsatisfactory

14. Suppose that you are conducting a conference-style training course for a group of 12   14._____
office assistants. Miss Jones is the only conferee who has not become involved in the discussion.
The BEST method of getting Miss Jones to participate is to

    A. ask her to comment on remarks made by the best-informed participant
    B. ask her to give a brief talk at the next session on a topic that interests her
    C. set up a role-play situation and assign her to take a part
    D. ask her a direct question which you know she can answer

15. Which of the following is NOT part of the *control* function of office management?   15._____

    A. Deciding on alternative courses of action
    B. Reporting periodically on productivity
    C. Evaluating performance against the standards
    D. Correcting deviations when required

16. Which of the following is NOT a principal aspect of the process of delegation?   16._____

    A. Developing improvements in methods used to carry out assignments
    B. Granting of permission to do what is necessary to carry out assignments

C. Assignment of duties by a supervisor to an immediate subordinate
D. Obligation on the part of a subordinate to carry out his assignment

17. Reluctance of a supervisor to delegate work effectively may be due to any or all of the following EXCEPT the supervisor's   17._____

A. unwillingness to take calculated risks
B. lack of confidence in subordinates
C. inability to give proper directions as to what he wants done
D. retention of ultimate responsibility for delegated work

18. A man cannot serve two masters.   18._____
This statement emphasizes the importance in an organization of following the principle of

A. specialization of work
B. unity of command
C. uniformity of assignment
D. span of control

19. In general, the number of subordinates an administrative assistant can supervise effectively tends to vary   19._____

A. *directly* with both similarity and complexity of their duties
B. *directly* with similarity of their duties and *inversely* with complexity of their duties
C. *inversely* with both similarity and complexity of their duties
D. *inversely* with similarity of their duties and *directly* with complexity of their duties

20. When an administrative assistant practices *general* rather than *close* supervision, which one of the following is MOST likely to happen?   20._____

A. His subordinates will not be as well-trained as employees who are supervised more closely.
B. Standards are likely to be lowered because subordinates will be under fewer pressures and will not be motivated to work toward set goals.
C. He will give fewer specific orders and spend more time on planning and coordinating than those supervisors who practice close supervision.
D. This supervisor will spend more time checking and correcting mistakes made by subordinates than would one who supervises closely.

Questions 21-25.

DIRECTIONS: Questions 21 to 25 are to be answered SOLELY on the basis of the information contained in the following paragraph.

Since an organization chart is pictorial in nature, there is a tendency for it to be drawn in an artistically balanced and appealing fashion, regardless of the realities of actual organizational structure. In addition to being subject to this distortion, there is the difficulty of communicating in any organization chart the relative importance or the relative size of various component parts of an organizational structure. Furthermore, because of the need for simplicity of design, an organization chart can never indicate the full extent of the interrelationships among the component parts of an organization. These interrelationships are often just as vital as the specifications which an organization chart endeavors to indicate. Yet, if an organization chart were to be drawn with all the wide variety of criss-crossing communication and cooperation networks existent within a typical organization, the chart would probably be much more confusing than informative. It is also obvious that no organization chart as such can 'prove' or 'disprove' that the organizational structure it represents is effective in realizing the objectives of the organization. At best, an organization chart can only illustrate some of the various factors to be taken into consideration in understanding, devising, or altering organizational arrangements.

21. According to the above paragraph, an organization chart can be expected to portray the   21.____

    A.   structure of the organization along somewhat ideal lines
    B.   relative size of the organizational units quite accurately
    C.   channels of information distribution within the organization graphically
    D.   extent of the obligation of each unit to meet the organizational objectives

22. According to the above paragraph, those aspects of internal functioning which are NOT   22.____
shown on an organization chart

    A.   can be considered to have little practical application in the operations of the organization
    B.   might well be considered to be as important as the structural relationships which a chart does present
    C.   could be the cause of considerable confusion in the operation of an organization which is quite large
    D.   would be most likely to provide the information needed to determine the overall effectiveness of an organization

23. In the above paragraph, the one of the following conditions which is NOT implied as   23.____
being a defect of an organization chart is that an organization chart may

    A.   present a picture of the organizational structure which is different from the structure that actually exists
    B.   fail to indicate the comparative size of various organizational units
    C.   be limited in its ability to convey some of the meaningful aspects of organizational relationships
    D.   become less useful over a period of time during which the organizational facts which it illustrated have changed

24. The one of the following which is the MOST suitable title for the above paragraph is   24.____

    A.   The Design and Construction of an Organization Chart
    B.   The Informal Aspects of an Organization Chart
    C.   The Inherent Deficiencies of an Organization Chart
    D.   The Utilization of a Typical Organization Chart

25. It can be INFERRED from the above paragraph that the function of an organization chart   25.____
is to

    A.   contribute to the comprehension of the organization form and arrangements
    B.   establish the capabilities of the organization to operate effectively
    C.   provide a balanced picture of the operations of the organization
    D.   eliminate the need for complexity in the organization's structure

KEY (CORRECT ANSWERS)

1.	D		11.	C
2.	C		12.	B
3.	D		13.	B
4.	B		14.	D
5.	A		15.	A
6.	C		16.	A
7.	B		17.	D
8.	A		18.	B
9.	A		19.	B
10.	D		20.	C

21.	A
22.	B
23.	D
24.	C
25.	A

TEST 3

DIRECTIONS: Each question or incomplete statement is followed by several suggested answers or completions. Select the one that BEST answers the question or completes the statement. *PRINT THE LETTER OF THE CORRECT ANSWER IN THE SPACE AT THE RIGHT.*

1. Of the following problems that might affect the conduct and outcome of an interview, the MOST troublesome and usually the MOST difficult for the interviewer to control is the

    A. tendency of the interviewee to anticipate the needs and preferences of the interviewer
    B. impulse to cut the interviewee off when he seems to have reached the end of an idea
    C. tendency of interviewee attitudes to bias the results
    D. tendency of the interviewer to do most of the talking

1.____

2. The administrative assistant MOST likely to be a good interviewer is one who

    A. is adept at manipulating people and circumstances toward his objectives
    B. is able to put himself in the position of the interviewee
    C. gets the more difficult questions out of the way at the beginning of the interview
    D. develops one style and technique that can be used in any type of interview

2.____

3. A good interviewer guards against the tendency to form an overall opinion about an interviewee on the basis of a single aspect of the interviewee's make-up.
This statement refers to a well-known source of error in interviewing known as the

    A. assumption error   B. expectancy error
    C. extension effect   D. halo effect

3.____

4. In conducting an *exit interview* with an employee who is leaving voluntarily, the interviewer's MAIN objective should be to

    A. see that the employee leaves with a good opinion of the organization
    B. learn the true reasons for the employee's resignation
    C. find out if the employee would consider a transfer
    D. try to get the employee to remain on the job

4.____

5. During an interview, an interviewee unexpectedly discloses a relevant but embarrassing personal fact.
It would be BEST for the interviewer to

    A. listen calmly, avoiding any gesture or facial expression that would suggest approval or disapproval of what is related
    B. change the subject, since further discussion in this area may reveal other embarrassing, but irrelevant, personal facts
    C. apologize to the interviewee for having led him to reveal such a fact and promise not to do so again
    D. bring the interview to a close as quickly as possible in order to avoid a discussion which may be distressful to the interviewee

5.____

6. Suppose that while you are interviewing an applicant for a position in your office, you notice a contradiction in facts in two of his responses.
For you to call the contradictions to his attention would be

    A. *inadvisable,* because it reduces the interviewee's level of participation
    B. *advisable,* because getting the facts is essential to a successful interview
    C. *inadvisable,* because the interviewer should use more subtle techniques to resolve any discrepancies
    D. *advisable,* because the interviewee should be impressed with the necessity for giving consistent answers

6.____

7. An interviewer should be aware that an undesirable result of including *leading questions* in an interview is to

    A. cause the interviewee to give *yes* or *no* answers with qualification or explanation
    B. encourage the interviewee to discuss irrelevant topics
    C. encourage the interviewee to give more meaningful information
    D. reduce the validity of the information obtained from the interviewee

7.____

8. The kind of interview which is PARTICULARLY helpful in getting an employee to tell about his complains and grievances is one in which

    A. a pattern has been worked out involving a sequence of exact questions to be asked
    B. the interviewee is expected to support his statements with specific evidence
    C. the interviewee is not made to answer specific questions but is encouraged to talk freely
    D. the interviewer has specific items on which he wishes to get or give information

8.____

9. Suppose you are scheduled to interview a student aide under your supervision concerning a health problem. You know that some of the questions you will be asking him will seem embarrassing to him, and that he may resist answering these questions.
In general, to hold these questions for the last part of the interview would be

    A. *desirable;* the intervening time period gives the interviewer an opportunity to plan how to ask these sensitive questions
    B. *undesirable;* the student aide will probably feel that he has been tricked when he suddenly must answer embarrassing questions
    C. *desirable;* the student aide will probably have increased confidence in the interviewer and be more willing to answer these questions
    D. *undesirable;* questions that are important should not be deferred until the end of the interview

9.____

10. The House passed an amendment to delete from the omnibus higher education bill a section that would have prohibited coeducational colleges and universities from considering sex as a factor in their admissions policy.
According to the above passage, consideration of sex as a factor in the admissions policy of coeducational colleges and universities would

    A. be permitted by the omnibus higher education bill if passed without further amendment
    B. be prohibited by the amendment to the omnibus higher education bill

10.____

C. have been prohibited by the deletion of a section from the omnibus higher education bill

D. have been permitted if the House had failed to pass the amendment

Questions 11-14.

DIRECTIONS: Answer Questions 11 to 14 only according to the information given in the passage below.

The proposition that administrative activity is essentially the same in all organizations appears to underlie some of the practices in the administration of private higher education. Although the practice is unusual in public education, there are numerous instances of industrial, governmental, or military administrators being assigned to private institutions of higher education and, to a lesser extent, of college and university presidents assuming administrative positions in other types of organizations. To test this theory that administrators are interchangeable, there is a need for systematic observation and classification. The myth that an educational administrator must first have experience in the teaching profession is firmly rooted in a long tradition that has historical prestige. The myth is bound up in the expectations of the public and personnel surrounding the administrator. Since administrative success depends significantly on how well an administrator meets the expectations others have of him, the myth may be more powerful than the special experience in helping the administrator attain organizational and educational objectives. Educational administrators who have risen through the teaching profession have often expressed nostalgia for the life of a teacher or scholar, but there is no evidence that this nostalgia contributes to administrative success.

11. Which of the following statements as completed is MOST consistent with the above passage?
The greatest number of administrators has moved from

A. industry and the military to government and universities
B. government and universities to industry and the military
C. government, the armed forces, and industry to colleges and universities
D. colleges and universities to government, the armed forces, and industry

11.____

12. Of the following, the MOST reasonable inference from the above passage is that a specific area requiring further research is the

A. place of myth in the tradition and history of the educational profession
B. relative effectiveness of educational administrators from inside and outside the teaching profession
C. performance of administrators in the administration of public colleges
D. degree of reality behind the nostalgia for scholarly pursuits often expressed by educational administrators

12.____

13. According to the above passage, the value to an educational administrator of experience in the teaching profession

A. lies in the firsthand knowledge he has acquired of immediate educational problems
B. may lie in the belief of his colleagues, subordinates, and the public that such experience is necessary

13.____

C. has been supported by evidence that the experience contributes to administrative success in educational fields

D. would be greater if the administrator were able to free himself from nostalgia for his former duties

14. Of the following, the MOST appropriate title for the above passage is   14.____

    A. Educational Administration, Its Problems
    B. The Experience Needed for Educational Administration
    C. Administration in Higher Education
    D. Evaluating Administrative Experience

Questions 15-20.

DIRECTIONS: Answer Questions 15 to 20 only according to the information contained in the following paragraph.

Methods of administration of office activities, much of which consists of providing information and 'know-how' needed to coordinate both activities within that particular office and other offices, have been among the last to come under the spotlight of management analysis. Progress has been rapid during the past decade, however, and is now accelerating at such a pace that an 'information revolution' in office management appears to be in the making. Although triggered by technological breakthroughs in electronic computers and other giant steps in mechanization, this information revolution must be attributed to underlying forces, such as the increased complexity of both governmental and private enterprise, and ever-keener competition. Size, diversification, specialization of function, and decentralization are among the forces which make coordination of activities both more imperative and more difficult. Increased competition, both domestic and international, leaves little margin for error in managerial decisions. Several developments during recent years indicate an evolving pattern. In 1960, the American Management Association expanded the scope of its activities and changed the name of its Office Management Division to Administrative Services Division. Also in 1960, the magazine Office Management merged with the magazine American Business, and this new publication was named Administrative Management.

15. A REASONABLE inference that can be made from the information in the above paragraph is that an important role of the office manager today is to   15.____

    A. work toward specialization of functions performed by his subordinates
    B. inform and train subordinates regarding any new developments in computer technology and mechanization
    C. assist the professional management analysts with the management analysis work in the organization
    D. supply information that can be used to help coordinate and manage the other activities of the organization

16. An IMPORTANT reason for the 'information revolution' that has been taking place in office management is the   16.____

    A. advance made in management analysis in the past decade
    B. technological breakthrough in electronic computers and mechanization
    C. more competitive and complicated nature of private business and government
    D. increased efficiency of office management techniques in the past ten years

17. According to the above paragraph, specialization of function in an organization is MOST   17.____
likely to result in

     A. the elimination of errors in managerial decisions
     B. greater need to coordinate activities
     C. more competition with other organizations, both domestic and international
     D. a need for office managers with greater flexibility

18. The word *evolving,* as used in the third from last sentence in the above paragraph,   18.____
means *most nearly*

     A. developing by gradual changes
     B. passing on to others
     C. occurring periodically
     D. breaking up into separate, constituent parts

19. Of the following, the MOST reasonable implication of the changes in names mentioned in   19.____
the last part of the above paragraph is that these groups are attempting to

     A. professionalize the field of office management and the title of Office Manager
     B. combine two publications into one because of the increased costs of labor and
        materials
     C. adjust to the fact that the field of office management is broadening
     D. appeal to the top managerial people rather than the office management people in
        business and government

20. According to the above paragraph, intense competition among domestic and interna-   20.____
tional enterprises makes it MOST important for an organization's managerial staff to

     A. coordinate and administer office activities with other activities in the organization
     B. make as few errors in decision-making as possible
     C. concentrate on decentralization and reduction of size of the individual divisions of
        the organization
     D. restrict decision-making only to top management officials

KEY (CORRECT ANSWERS)

1.	A		11.	C
2.	B		12.	B
3.	D		13.	B
4.	B		14.	B
5.	A		15.	D
6.	B		16.	C
7.	D		17.	B
8.	C		18.	A
9.	C		19.	C
10.	A		20.	B

———

RECORD KEEPING
EXAMINATION SECTION
TEST 1

DIRECTIONS: Each question or incomplete statement is followed by several suggested answers or completions. Select the one that BEST answers the question or completes the statement. *PRINT THE LETTER OF THE CORRECT ANSWER IN THE SPACE AT THE RIGHT.*

Questions 1-15.

DIRECTIONS: Questions 1 through 15 are to be answered on the basis of the following list of company names below. Arrange a file alphabetically, word-by-word, disregarding punctuation, conjunctions, and apostrophes. Then answer the questions.

A Bee C Reading Materials
ABCO Parts
A Better Course for Test Preparation
AAA Auto Parts Co.
A-Z Auto Parts, Inc.
Aabar Books
Abbey, Joanne
Boman-Sylvan Law Firm
BMW Autowerks
C Q Service Company
Chappell-Murray, Inc.
E&E Life Insurance
Emcrisco
Gigi Arts
Gordon, Jon & Associates
SOS Plumbing
Schmidt, J.B. Co.

1. Which of these files should appear FIRST?   1._____

    A. ABCO Parts
    B. A Bee C Reading Materials
    C. A Better Course for Test Preparation
    D. AAA Auto Parts Co.

2. Which of these files should appear SECOND?   2._____

    A. A-Z Auto Parts, Inc.
    B. A Bee C Reading Materials
    C. A Better Course for Test Preparation
    D. AAA Auto Parts Co.

3. Which of these files should appear THIRD?   3._____

    A. ABCO Parts
    B. A Bee C Reading Materials
    C. Aabar Books
    D. AAA Auto Parts Co.

4. Which of these files should appear FOURTH?   4.____

    A. Aabar Books
    B. ABCO Parts
    C. Abbey, Joanne
    D. AAA Auto Parts Co.

5. Which of these files should appear LAST?   5.____

    A. Gordon, Jon & Associates
    B. Gigi Arts
    C. Schmidt, J.B. Co.
    D. SOS Plumbing

6. Which of these files should appear between A-Z Auto Parts, Inc. and Abbey, Joanne?   6.____

    A. A Bee C Reading Materials
    B. AAA Auto Parts Co.
    C. ABCO Parts
    D. A Better Course for Test Preparation

7. Which of these files should appear between ABCO Parts and Aabar Books?   7.____

    A. A Bee C Reading Materials
    B. Abbey, Joanne
    C. Aabar Books
    D. A-Z Auto Parts

8. Which of these files should appear between Abbey, Joanne and Boman-Sylvan Law   8.____
    Firm?

    A. A Better Course for Test Preparation
    B. BMW Autowerks
    C. Chappell-Murray, Inc.
    D. Aabar Books

9. Which of these files should appear between Abbey, Joanne and C Q Service?   9.____

    A. A-Z Auto Parts,Inc.   B. BMW Autowerks
    C. Choices A and B   D. Chappell-Murray, Inc.

10. Which of these files should appear between C Q Service Company and Emcrisco?   10.____

    A. Chappell-Murray, Inc.   B. E&E Life Insurance
    C. Gigi Arts   D. Choices A and B

11. Which of these files should NOT appear between C Q Service Company and E&E Life   11.____
    Insurance?

    A. Gordon, Jon & Associates
    B. Emcrisco
    C. Gigi Arts
    D. All of the above

12. Which of these files should appear between Chappell-Murray Inc., and Gigi Arts? 12.____

    A. CQ Service Inc. E&E Life Insurance, and Emcrisco
    B. Emcrisco, E&E Life Insurance, and Gordon, Jon & Associates
    C. E&E Life Insurance and Emcrisco
    D. Emcrisco and Gordon, Jon & Associates

13. Which of these files should appear between Gordon, Jon & Associates and SOS Plumb- 13.____
ing?

    A. Gigi Arts   B. Schmidt, J.B. Co.
    C. Choices A and B   D. None of the above

14. Each of the choices lists the four files in their proper alphabetical order except 14.____

    A. E&E Life Insurance; Gigi Arts; Gordon, Jon & Associates; SOS Plumbing
    B. E&E Life Insurance; Emcrisco; Gigi Arts; SOS Plumbing
    C. Emcrisco; Gordon, Jon & Associates; SOS Plumbing; Schmidt, J.B. Co.
    D. Emcrisco; Gigi Arts; Gordon, Jon & Associates; SOS Plumbing

15. Which of the choices lists the four files in their proper alphabetical order? 15.____

    A. Gigi Arts; Gordon, Jon & Associates; SOS Plumbing; Schmidt, J.B. Co.
    B. Gordon, Jon & Associates; Gigi Arts; Schmidt, J.B. Co.; SOS Plumbing
    C. Gordon, Jon & Associates; Gigi Arts; SOS Plumbing; Schmidt, J.B. Co.
    D. Gigi Arts; Gordon, Jon & Associates; Schmidt, J.B. Co.; SOS Plumbing

16. The alphabetical filing order of two businesses with identical names is determined by the 16.____

    A. length of time each business has been operating
    B. addresses of the businesses
    C. last name of the company president
    D. none of the above

17. In an alphabetical filing system, if a business name includes a number, it should be 17.____

    A. disregarded
    B. considered a number and placed at the end of an alphabetical section
    C. treated as though it were written in words and alphabetized accordingly
    D. considered a number and placed at the beginning of an alphabetical section

18. If a business name includes a contraction (such as *don't* or *it's*), how should that word be 18.____
treated in an alphabetical filing system?

    A. Divide the word into its separate parts and treat it as two words.
    B. Ignore the letters that come after the apostrophe.
    C. Ignore the word that contains the contraction.
    D. Ignore the apostrophe and consider all letters in the contraction.

19. In what order should the parts of an address be considered when using an alphabetical 19.____
filing system?

    A. City or town; state; street name; house or building number
    B. State; city or town; street name; house or building number
    C. House or building number; street name; city or town; state
    D. Street name; city or town; state

20. A business record should be cross-referenced when a(n)   20._____

    A. organization is known by an abbreviated name
    B. business has a name change because of a sale, incorporation, or other reason
    C. business is known by a *coined* or common name which differs from a dictionary spelling
    D. all of the above

21. A geographical filing system is MOST effective when   21._____

    A. location is more important than name
    B. many names or titles sound alike
    C. dealing with companies who have offices all over the world
    D. filing personal and business files

Questions 22-25.

DIRECTIONS: Questions 22 through 25 are to be answered on the basis of the list of items below, which are to be filed geographically. Organize the items geographically and then answer the questions.
    1. University Press at Berkeley, U.S.
    2. Maria Sanchez, Mexico City, Mexico
    3. Great Expectations Ltd. in London, England
    4. Justice League, Cape Town, South Africa, Africa
    5. Crown Pearls Ltd. in London, England
    6. Joseph Prasad in London, England

22. Which of the following arrangements of the items is composed according to the policy of: 22._____
Continent, Country, City, Firm or Individual Name?

    A. 5, 3, 4, 6, 2, 1   B. 4, 5, 3, 6, 2, 1
    C. 1, 4, 5, 3, 6, 2   D. 4, 5, 3, 6, 1, 2

23. Which of the following files is arranged according to the policy of: *Continent, Country,* 23._____
City, Firm or Individual Name?

    A. South Africa. Africa. Cape Town. Justice League
    B. Mexico. Mexico City, Maria Sanchez
    C. North America. United States. Berkeley. University Press
    D. England. Europe. London. Prasad, Joseph

24. Which of the following arrangements of the items is composed according to the policy of: 24._____
Country, City, Firm or Individual Name?

    A. 5, 6, 3, 2, 4, 1   B. 1, 5, 6, 3, 2, 4
    C. 6, 5, 3, 2, 4, 1   D. 5, 3, 6, 2, 4, 1

25. Which of the following files is arranged according to a policy of: *Country, City, Firm or* 25._____
Individual Name?

    A. England. London. Crown Pearls Ltd.
    B. North America. United States. Berkeley. University Press
    C. Africa. Cape Town. Justice League
    D. Mexico City. Mexico. Maria Sanchez

26. Under which of the following circumstances would a phonetic filing system be MOST effective?   26._____

    A. When the person in charge of filing can't spell very well
    B. With large files with names that sound alike
    C. With large files with names that are spelled alike
    D. All of the above

Questions 27-29.

DIRECTIONS: Questions 27 through 29 are to be answered on the basis of the following list of numerical files.
    1. 391-023-100
    2. 361-132-170
    3. 385-732-200
    4. 381-432-150
    5. 391-632-387
    6. 361-423-303
    7. 391-123-271

27. Which of the following arrangements of the files follows a consecutive-digit system?   27._____

    A. 2, 3, 4, 1   B. 1, 5, 7, 3
    C. 2, 4, 3, 1   D. 3, 1, 5, 7

28. Which of the following arrangements follows a terminal-digit system?   28._____

    A. 1, 7, 2, 4, 3   B. 2, 1, 4, 5, 7
    C. 7, 6, 5, 4, 3   D. 1, 4, 2, 3, 7

29. Which of the following lists follows a middle-digit system?   29._____

    A. 1, 7, 2, 6, 4, 5, 3   B. 1, 2, 7, 4, 6, 5, 3
    C. 7, 2, 1, 3, 5, 6, 4   D. 7, 1, 2, 4, 6, 5, 3

Questions 30-31.

DIRECTIONS: Questions 30 and 31 are to be answered on the basis of the following information.
    1. Reconfirm Laura Bates appointment with James Caldecort on December 12 at 9:30 A.M.
    2. Laurence Kinder contact Julia Lucas on August 3 and set up a meeting for week of September 23 at 4 P.M.
    3. John Lutz contact Larry Waverly on August 3 and set up appointment for September 23 at 9:30 A.M.
    4. Call for tickets for Gerry Stanton August 21 for New Jersey on September 23, flight 143 at 4:43 P.M.

30. A chronological file for the above information would be   30._____

    A. 4, 3, 2, 1   B. 3, 2, 4, 1
    C. 4, 2, 3, 1   D. 3, 1, 2, 4

31. Using the above information, a chronological file for the date of September 23 would be   31._____

    A. 2, 3, 4   B. 3, 1, 4   C. 3, 2, 4   D. 4, 3, 2

Questions 32-34.

DIRECTIONS: Questions 32 through 34 are to be answered on the basis of the following infor-
              mation.
    1. Call Roger Epstein, Ashoke Naipaul, Jon Anderson, and Sarah Washington on
        April 19 at 1:00 P.M. to set up meeting with Alika D'Ornay for June 6 in New York.
    2. Call Martin Ames before noon on April 19 to confirm afternoon meeting with Bob
        Greenwood on April 20th
    3. Set up meeting room at noon for 2:30 P.M. meeting on April 19th;
    4. Ashley Stanton contact Bob Greenwood at 9:00 A.M. on April 20 and set up meet-
        ing for June 6 at 8:30 A.M.
    5. Carol Guiland contact Shelby Van Ness during afternoon of April 20 and set up
        meeting for June 6 at 10:00 A.M.
    6. Call airline and reserve tickets on June 6 for Roger Epstein trip *to* Denver on July 8
    7. Meeting at 2:30 P.M. on April 19th

32. A chronological file for all of the above information would be   32._____

    A. 2, 1, 3, 7, 5, 4, 6   B. 3, 7, 2, 1, 4, 5, 6
    C. 3, 7, 1, 2, 5, 4, 6   D. 2, 3, 1, 7, 4, 5, 6

33. A chronological file for the date of April 19th would be   33._____

    A. 2, 3, 7, 1   B. 2, 3, 1, 7
    C. 7, 1, 3, 2   D. 3, 7, 1, 2

34. Add the following information to the file, and then create a chronological file for April 20th: 34._____
    8. April 20: 3:00 P.M. meeting between Bob Greenwood and Martin Ames.

    A. 4, 5, 8   B. 4, 8, 5   C. 8, 5, 4   D. 5, 4, 8

35. The PRIMARY advantage of computer records filing over a manual system is   35._____

    A. speed of retrieval   B. accuracy
    C. cost   D. potential file loss

KEY (CORRECT ANSWERS)

1.	B		16.	B
2.	C		17.	C
3.	D		18.	D
4.	A		19.	A
5.	D		20.	D
6.	C		21.	A
7.	B		22.	B
8.	B		23.	C
9.	C		24.	D
10.	D		25.	A
11.	D		26.	B
12.	C		27.	C
13.	B		28.	D
14.	C		29.	A
15.	D		30.	B

31.	C
32.	D
33.	B
34.	A
35.	A

READING COMPREHENSION
UNDERSTANDING AND INTERPRETING WRITTEN MATERIAL
EXAMINATION SECTION
TEST 1

DIRECTIONS: Each question or incomplete statement is followed by several suggested answers or completions. Select the one that BEST answers the question or completes the statement. *PRINT THE LETTER OF THE CORRECT ANSWER IN THE SPACE AT THE RIGHT.*

Questions 1-5.

DIRECTIONS: Questions 1 through 5 are to be answered SOLELY on the basis of the following passage.

The most effective control mechanism to prevent gross incompetence on the part of public employees is a good personnel program. The personnel officer in the line departments and the central personnel agency should exert positive leadership to raise levels of performance. Although the key factor is the quality of the personnel recruited, staff members other than personnel officers can make important contributions to efficiency. Administrative analysts, now employed in many agencies, make detailed studies of organization and procedures, with the purpose of eliminating delays, waste, and other inefficiencies. Efficiency is, however, more than a question of good organization and procedures; it is also the product of the attitudes and values of the public employees. Personal motivation can provide the will to be efficient. The best management studies will not result in substantial improvement of the performance of those employees who feel no great urge to work up to their abilities.

1.   The above passage indicates that the KEY factor in preventing gross incompetence of public employees is the   1.____

    A.   hiring of administrative analysts to assist personnel people
    B.   utilization of effective management studies
    C.   overlapping of responsibility
    D.   quality of the employees hired

2.   According to the above passage, the central personnel agency staff SHOULD   2.____

    A.   work more closely with administrative analysts in the line departments than with personnel officers
    B.   make a serious effort to avoid jurisdictional conflicts with personnel officers in line departments
    C.   contribute to improving the quality of work of public employees
    D.   engage in a comprehensive program to change the public's negative image of public employees

3.   The above passage indicates that efficiency in an organization can BEST be brought about by   3.____

    A.   eliminating ineffective control mechanisms
    B.   instituting sound organizational procedures

C. promoting competent personnel
D. recruiting people with desire to do good work

4. According to the above passage, the purpose of administrative analysis in a public agency is to

    4.____

  A. prevent injustice to the public employee
  B. promote the efficiency of the agency
  C. protect the interests of the public
  D. ensure the observance of procedural due process

5. The above passage implies that a considerable rise in the quality of work of public employees can be brought about by

    5.____

  A. encouraging positive employee attitudes toward work
  B. controlling personnel officers who exceed their powers
  C. creating warm personal associations among public employees in an agency
  D. closing loopholes in personnel organization and procedures

Questions 6-8.

DIRECTIONS: Questions 6 through 8 are to be answered SOLELY on the basis of the following passage on Employee Needs.

EMPLOYEE NEEDS

The greatest waste in industry and in government may be that of human resources. This waste usually derives not from employees' unwillingness or inability, but from management's ineptness to meet the maintenance and motivational needs of employees. Maintenance needs refer to such needs as providing employees with safe places to work, written work rules, job security, adequate salary, employer-sponsored social activities, and with knowledge of their role in the overall framework of the organization. However, of greatest significance to employees are the motivational needs of job growth, achievement, responsibility, and recognition.

Although employee dissatisfaction may stem from either poor maintenance or poor motivation factors, the outward manifestation of the dissatisfaction may be very much alike, i.e., negativism, complaints, deterioration of performance, and so forth. The improvement in the lighting of an employee's work area or raising his level of pay won't do much good if the source of the dissatisfaction is the absence of a meaningful assignment. By the same token, if an employee is dissatisfied with what he considers inequitable pay, the introduction of additional challenge in his work may simply make matters worse.

It is relatively easy for an employee to express frustration by complaining about pay, washroom conditions, fringe benefits, and so forth; but most people cannot easily express resentment in terms of the more abstract concepts concerning job growth, responsibility, and achievement.

It would be wrong to assume that there is no interaction between maintenance and motivational needs of employees. For example, conditions of high motivation often overshadow poor maintenance conditions. If an organization is in a period of strong growth and expansion, opportunities for job growth, responsibility, recognition, and achievement are usually abundant, but the rapid growth may have outrun the upkeep of maintenance factors. In this situation, motivation may be high, but only if employees recognize the poor maintenance conditions as unavoidable and temporary. The subordination of maintenance factors cannot go on indefinitely, even with the highest motivation.

Both maintenance and motivation factors influence the behavior of all employees, but employees are not identical and, furthermore, the needs of any individual do not remain constant. However, a broad distinction can be made between employees who have a basic orientation toward maintenance factors and those with greater sensitivity toward motivation factors.

A highly maintenance-oriented individual, preoccupied with the factors peripheral to his job rather than the job itself, is more concerned with comfort than challenge. He does not get deeply involved with his work but does with the condition of his work area, toilet facilities, and his time for going to lunch. By contrast, a strongly motivation-oriented employee is usually relatively indifferent to his surroundings and is caught up in the pursuit of work goals.

Fortunately, there are few people who are either exclusively maintenance-oriented or purely motivation-oriented. The former would be deadwood in an organization, while the latter might trample on those around him in his pursuit to achieve his goals.

6. With respect to employee motivational and maintenance needs, the management poli-   6._____
    cies of an organization which is growing rapidly will probably result

    A. more in meeting motivational needs rather than maintenance needs
    B. more in meeting maintenance needs rather than motivational needs
    C. in meeting both of these needs equally
    D. in increased effort to define the motivational and maintenance needs of its employ-
        ees

7. In accordance with the above passage, which of the following CANNOT be considered   7._____
    as an example of an employee maintenance need for railroad clerks?

    A. Providing more relief periods
    B. Providing fair salary increases at periodic intervals
    C. Increasing job responsibilities
    D. Increasing health insurance benefits

8. Most employees in an organization may be categorized as being interested in   8._____

    A. maintenance needs *only*
    B. motivational needs *only*
    C. both motivational and maintenance needs
    D. money only, to the exclusion of all other needs

Questions 9-11.

DIRECTIONS: Questions 9 through 11 are to be answered SOLELY on the basis of the follow-
               ing passage on Good Employee Practices.

GOOD EMPLOYEE PRACTICES

As a city employee, you will be expected to take an interest in your work and perform the duties of your job to the best of your ability and in a spirit of cooperation. Nothing shows an interest in your work more than coming to work on time, not only at the start of the day but also when returning from lunch. If it is necessary for you to keep a personal appointment at lunch hour which might cause a delay in getting back to work on time, you should explain the situation to your supervisor and get his approval to come back a little late before you leave for lunch.

You should do everything that is asked of you willingly and consider important even the small jobs that your supervisor gives you. Although these jobs may seem unimportant, if you forget to do them or if you don't do them right, trouble may develop later.

Getting along well with your fellow workers will add much to the enjoyment of your work. You should respect your fellow workers and try to see their side when a disagreement arises. The better you get along with your fellow workers and your supervisor, the better you will like your job and the better you will be able to do it.

9. According to the above passage, in your job as a city employee, you are expected to   9._____

    A.   show a willingness to cooperate on the job
    B.   get your supervisor's approval before keeping any personal appointments at lunch hour
    C.   avoid doing small jobs that seem unimportant
    D.   do the easier jobs at the start of the day and the more difficult ones later on

10. According to the above passage, getting to work on time shows that you   10._____

    A.   need the job
    B.   have an interest in your work
    C.   get along well with your fellow workers
    D.   like your supervisor

11. According to the above passage, the one of the following statements that is NOT true is   11._____

    A.   if you do a small job wrong, trouble may develop
    B.   you should respect your fellow workers
    C.   if you disagree with a fellow worker, you should try to see his side of the story
    D.   the less you get along with your supervisor, the better you will be able to do your job

Questions 12-15.

DIRECTIONS: Questions 12 through 15 are to be answered SOLELY on the basis of the following passage on Employee Suggestions.

EMPLOYEE SUGGESTIONS

To increase the effectiveness of the city government, the city asks its employees to offer suggestions when they feel an improvement could be made in some government operation. The Employees' Suggestions Program was started to encourage city employees to do this.

Through this Program, which is only for city employees, cash awards may be given to those whose suggestions are submitted and approved. Suggestions are looked for not only from supervisors but from all city employees as any city employee may get an idea which might be approved and contribute greatly to the solution of some problem of city government

Therefore, all suggestions for improvement are welcome, whether they be suggestions on how to improve working conditions, or on how to increase the speed with which work is done, or on how to reduce or eliminate such things as waste, time losses, accidents or fire hazards. There are, however, a few types of suggestions for which cash awards cannot be given. An example of this type would be a suggestion to increase salaries or a suggestion to change the regulations about annual leave or about sick leave. The number of suggestions sent in has increased sharply during the past few years. It is hoped that it will keep increasing in the future in order to meet the city's needs for more ideas for improved ways of doing things.

12. According to the above passage, the MAIN reason why the city asks its employees for suggestions about government operations is to   12.____

    A. increase the effectiveness of the city government
    B. show that the Employees' Suggestion Program is working well
    C. show that everybody helps run the city government
    D. have the employee win a prize

13. According to the above passage, the Employees' Suggestion Program can approve awards ONLY for those suggestions that come from   13.____

    A. city employees
    B. city employees who are supervisors
    C. city employees who are not supervisors
    D. experienced employees of the city

14. According to the above passage, a cash award cannot be given through the Employees' Suggestion Program for a suggestion about   14.____

    A. getting work done faster
    B. helping prevent accidents on the job
    C. increasing the amount of annual leave for city employees
    D. reducing the chance of fire where city employees work

15. According to the above passage, the suggestions sent in during the past few years have   15.____

    A. all been approved
    B. generally been well written
    C. been mostly about reducing or eliminating waste
    D. been greater in number than before

Questions 16-18.

DIRECTIONS: Questions 16 through 18 are to be answered SOLELY on the basis of the following passage.

The supervisor will gain the respect of the members of his staff and increase his influence over them by controlling his temper and avoiding criticizing anyone publicly. When a mistake is made, the good supervisor will talk it over with the employee quietly and privately. The supervisor will listen to the employee's story, suggest the better way of doing the job, and offer help so the mistake won't happen again. Before closing the discussion, the supervisor should try to find something good to say about other parts of the employee's work. Some praise and appreciation, along with instruction, is more likely to encourage an employee to improve in those areas where he is weakest.

16. A good title that would show the meaning of the above passage would be 16.____

    A. HOW TO CORRECT EMPLOYEE ERRORS
    B. HOW TO PRAISE EMPLOYEES
    C. MISTAKES ARE PREVENTABLE
    D. THE WEAK EMPLOYEE

17. According to the above passage, the work of an employee who has made a mistake is more likely to improve if the supervisor 17.____

    A. avoids criticizing him
    B. gives him a chance to suggest a better way of doing the work
    C. listens to the employee's excuses to see if he is right
    D. praises good work at the same time he corrects the mistake

18. According to the above passage, when a supervisor needs to correct an employee's mistake, it is important that he 18.____

    A. allow some time to go by after the mistake is made
    B. do so when other employees are not present
    C. show his influence with his tone of voice
    D. tell other employees to avoid the same mistake

Questions 19-23.

DIRECTIONS: Questions 19 through 23 are to be answered SOLELY on the basis of the following passage.

In studying the relationships of people to the organizational structure, it is absolutely necessary to identify and recognize the informal organizational structure. These relationships are necessary when coordination of a plan is attempted. They may be with *the boss,* line supervisors, staff personnel, or other representatives of the formal organization's hierarchy, and they may include the *liaison men* who serve as the leaders of the informal organization. An acquaintanceship with the people serving in these roles in the organization, and its formal counterpart, permits a supervisor to recognize sensitive areas in which it is simple to get a conflict reaction. Avoidance of such areas, plus conscious efforts to inform other people of his own objectives for various plans, will usually enlist their aid and support. Planning *without people* can lead to disaster because the individuals who must act together to make any plan a success are more important than the plans themselves.

19. Of the following titles, the one that MOST clearly describes the above passage is 19.____

    A. COORDINATION OF A FUNCTION
    B. AVOIDANCE OF CONFLICT
    C. PLANNING WITH PEOPLE
    D. PLANNING OBJECTIVES

20. According to the above passage, attempts at coordinating plans may fail unless   20._____

    A. the plan's objectives are clearly set forth
    B. conflict between groups is resolved
    C. the plans themselves are worthwhile
    D. informal relationships are recognized

21. According to the above passage, conflict   21._____

    A. may, in some cases, be desirable to secure results
    B. produces more heat than light
    C. should be avoided at all costs
    D. possibilities can be predicted by a sensitive supervisor

22. The above passage implies that   22._____

    A. informal relationships are more important than formal structure
    B. the weakness of a formal structure depends upon informal relationships
    C. liaison men are the key people to consult when taking formal and informal structures into account
    D. individuals in a group are at least as important as the plans for the group

23. The above passage suggests that   23._____

    A. some planning can be disastrous
    B. certain people in sensitive areas should be avoided
    C. the supervisor should discourage acquaintanceships in the organization
    D. organizational relationships should be consciously limited

Questions 24-25.

DIRECTIONS: Questions 24 and 25 are to be answered SOLELY on the basis of the following passage.

Good personnel relations of an organization depend upon mutual confidence, trust, and good will. The basis of confidence is understanding. Most troubles start with people who do not understand each other. When the organization's intentions or motives are misunderstood, or when reasons for actions, practices, or policies are misconstrued, complete cooperation from individuals is not forthcoming. If management expects full cooperation from employees, it has a responsibility of sharing with them the information which is the foundation of proper understanding, confidence, and trust. Personnel management has long since outgrown the days when it was the vogue to *treat them rough and tell them nothing.* Up-to-date personnel management provides all possible information about the activities, aims, and purposes of the organization. It seems altogether creditable that a desire should exist among employees for such information which the best-intentioned executive might think would not interest them and which the worst-intentioned would think was none of their business.

24. The above passage implies that one of the causes of the difficulty which an organization   24._____
might have with its personnel relations is that its employees

    A. have not expressed interest in the activities, aims, and purposes of the organization
    B. do not believe in the good faith of the organization

C. have not been able to give full cooperation to the organization
D. do not recommend improvements in the practices and policies of the organization

25. According to the above passage, in order for an organization to have good personnel relations, it is NOT essential that   25.____

A. employees have confidence in the organization
B. the purposes of the organization be understood by the employees
C. employees have a desire for information about the organization
D. information about the organization be communicated to employees

---

KEY (CORRECT ANSWERS)

1. D		11. D
2. C		12. A
3. D		13. A
4. B		14. C
5. A		15. D
6. A		16. A
7. C		17. D
8. C		18. B
9. A		19. C
10. B		20. D

21. D
22. D
23. A
24. B
25. C

TEST 2

Questions 1-8.

DIRECTIONS: Questions 1 through 8 are to be answered SOLELY on the basis of the following passage.

Important figures in education and in public affairs have recommended development of a private organization sponsored in part by various private foundations which would offer installment payment plans to full-time matriculated students in accredited colleges and universities in the United States and Canada. Contracts would be drawn to cover either tuition and fees, or tuition, fees, room and board in college facilities, from one year up to and including six years. A special charge, which would vary with the length of the contract, would be added to the gross repayable amount. This would be in addition to interest at a rate which would vary with the income of the parents. There would be a 3% annual interest charge for families with total income, before income taxes, of $50,000 or less. The rate would increase by 1/10 of 1% for every $1,000 of additional net income in excess of $50,000 up to a maximum of 10% interest. Contracts would carry an insurance provision on the life of the parent or guardian who signs the contract; all contracts must have the signature of a parent or guardian. Payment would be scheduled in equal monthly installments.

1. Which of the following students would be eligible for the payment plan described in the above passage? A

    A. matriculated student taking six semester hours toward a graduate degree
    B. matriculated student taking seventeen semester hours toward an undergraduate degree
    C. graduate matriculated at the University of Mexico taking eighteen semester hours toward a graduate degree
    D. student taking eighteen semester hours in a special pre-matriculation program

1.____

2. According to the above passage, the organization described would be sponsored in part by

    A. private foundations
    B. colleges and universities
    C. persons in the field of education
    D. persons in public life

2.____

3. Which of the following expenses could NOT be covered by a contract with the organization described in the above passage?

    A. Tuition amounting to $20,000 per year
    B. Registration and laboratory fees
    C. Meals at restaurants near the college
    D. Rent for an apartment in a college dormitory

3.____

4. The total amount to be paid would include ONLY the

    A. principal
    B. principal and interest
    C. principal, interest, and special charge
    D. principal, interest, special charge, and fee

4.____

5. The contract would carry insurance on the   5.____

    A. life of the student
    B. life of the student's parents
    C. income of the parents of the student
    D. life of the parent who signed the contract

6. The interest rate for an annual loan of $25,000 from the organization described in the   6.____
above passage for a student whose family's net income was $55,000 should be

    A. 3%   B. 3.5%   C. 4%   D. 4.5%

7. The interest rate for an annual loan of $35,000 from the organization described in the   7.____
above passage for a student whose family's net income was $100,000 should be

    A. 5%   B. 8%   C. 9%   D. 10%

8. John Lee has submitted an application for the installment payment plan described in the   8.____
above passage. John's mother and father have a store which grossed $500,000 last
year, but the income which the family received from the store was $90,000 before taxes.
They also had $5,000 income from stock dividends. They paid $10,000 in income taxes.
The amount of income upon which the interest should be based is

    A. $85,000   B. $90,000   C. $95,000   D. $105,000

Questions 9-13.

DIRECTIONS: Questions 9 through 13 are to be answered SOLELY on the basis of the follow-
                 ing passage.

Since an organization chart is pictorial in nature, there is a tendency for it to be drawn in
an artistically balanced and appealing fashion, regardless of the realities of actual organizational structure. In addition to being subject to this distortion, there is the difficulty of communicating in any organization chart the relative importance or the relative size of various
component parts of an organizational structure. Furthermore, because of the need for simplicity of design, an organization chart can never indicate the full extent of the interrelationships among the component parts of an organization.

These interrelationships are often just as vital as the specifications which an organization
chart endeavors to indicate. Yet, if an organization chart were to be drawn with all the wide
variety of criss-crossing communication and cooperation networks existent within a typical
organization, the chart would probably be much more confusing than informative. It is also
obvious that no organization chart as such can prove or disprove that the organizational
structure it represents is effective in realizing the objectives of the organization. At best, an
organization chart can only illustrate some of the various factors to be taken into consideration in understanding, devising, or altering organizational arrangements.

9. According to the above passage, an organization chart can be expected to portray the   9.____

    A. structure of the organization along somewhat ideal lines
    B. relative size of the organizational units quite accurately
    C. channels of information distribution within the organization graphically
    D. extent of the obligation of each unit to meet the organizational objectives

10. According to the above passage, those aspects of internal functioning which are NOT   10.____
    shown on an organization chart

    A. can be considered to have little practical application in the operations of the organi-
       zation
    B. might well be considered to be as important as the structural relationships which a
       chart does present
    C. could be the cause of considerable confusion in the operations of an organization
       which is quite large
    D. would be most likely to provide the information needed to determine the overall
       effectiveness of an organization

11. In the above passage, the one of the following conditions which is NOT implied as being   11.____
    a defect of an organization chart is that an organization chart may

    A. present a picture of the organizational structure which is different from the struc-
       ture that actually exists
    B. fail to indicate the comparative size of various organizational units
    C. be limited in its ability to convey some of the meaningful aspects of organizational
       relationships
    D. become less useful over a period of time during which the organizational facts
       which it illustrated have changed

12. The one of the following which is the MOST suitable title for the above passage is   12.____

    A. THE DESIGN AND CONSTRUCTION OF AN ORGANIZATION CHART
    B. THE INFORMAL ASPECTS OF AN ORGANIZATION CHART
    C. THE INHERENT DEFICIENCIES OF AN ORGANIZATION CHART
    D. THE UTILIZATION OF A TYPICAL ORGANIZATION CHART

13. It can be INFERRED from the above passage that the function of an organization chart is   13.____
    to

    A. contribute to the comprehension of the organization form and arrangements
    B. establish the capabilities of the organization to operate effectively
    C. provide a balanced picture of the operations of the organization
    D. eliminate the need for complexity in the organization's structure

Questions 14-16.

DIRECTIONS: Questions 14 through 16 are to be answered SOLELY on the basis of the fol-
              lowing passage.

    In dealing with visitors to the school office, the school secretary must use initiative, tact,
and good judgment. All visitors should be greeted promptly and courteously. The nature of
their business should be determined quickly and handled expeditiously. Frequently, the secretary should be able to handle requests, receipts, deliveries, or passes herself. Her judgment
should determine when a visitor should see members of the staff or the principal. Serious
problems or doubtful cases should be referred to a supervisor.

14. In general, visitors should be handled by the   14.____

     A. school secretary   B. principal
     C. appropriate supervisor   D. person who is free

15. It is wise to obtain the following information from visitors: 15.____

     A. Name   B. Nature of business
     C. Address   D. Problems they have

16. All visitors who wish to see members of the staff should   16.____

     A. be permitted to do so
     B. produce identification
     C. do so for valid reasons only
     D. be processed by a supervisor

Questions 17-19.

DIRECTIONS: Questions 17 through 19 are to be answered SOLELY on the basis of the following passage.

Information regarding payroll status, salary differentials, promotional salary increments, deductions, and pension payments should be given to all members of the staff who have questions regarding these items. On occasion, if the secretary is uncertain regarding the information, the staff member should be referred to the principal or the appropriate agency. No question by a staff member regarding payroll status should be brushed aside as immaterial or irrelevant. The school secretary must always try to handle the question or pass it on to the person who can handle it.

17. If a teacher is dissatisfied with information regarding her salary status, as given by the school secretary, the matter should be   17.____

     A. dropped
     B. passed on to the principal
     C. passed on by the secretary to proper agency or the principal
     D. made a basis for grievance procedures

18. The following is an adequate summary of the above passage: 18.____

     A. The secretary must handle all payroll matters
     B. The secretary must handle all payroll matters or know who can handle them
     C. The secretary or the principal must handle all payroll matters
     D. Payroll matters too difficult to handle must be followed up until they are solved

19. The above passage implies that   19.____

     A. many teachers ask immaterial questions regarding payroll status
     B. few teachers ask irrelevant pension questions
     C. no teachers ask immaterial salary questions
     D. no question regarding salary should be considered irrelevant

Questions 20-22.

DIRECTIONS: Questions 20 through 22 are to be answered SOLELY on the basis of the following passage.

The necessity for good speech on the part of the school secretary cannot be overstated. The school secretary must deal with the general public, the pupils, the members of the staff, and the school supervisors. In every situation which involves the general public, the secretary serves as a representative of the school. In dealing with pupils, the secretary's speech must serve as a model from which students may guide themselves. Slang, colloquialisms, malapropisms, and local dialects must be avoided.

20. The above passage implies that the speech pattern of the secretary must be   20._____

    A. perfect
    B. very good
    C. average
    D. on a level with that of the pupils

21. The last sentence indicates that slang   21._____

    A. is acceptable
    B. occurs in all speech
    C. might be used occasionally
    D. should be shunned

22. The above passage implies that the speech of pupils   22._____

    A. may be influenced   B. does not change readily
    C. is generally good   D. is generally poor

Questions 23-25.

DIRECTIONS: Questions 23 through 25 are to be answered SOLELY on the basis of the following passage.

The school secretary who is engaged in the task of filing records and correspondence should follow a general set of rules. Items which are filed should be available to other secretaries or to supervisors quickly and easily by means of the application of a modicum of common sense and good judgment. Items which, by their nature, may be difficult to find should be cross-indexed. Folders and drawers should be neatly and accurately labeled. There should never be a large accumulation of papers which have not been filed.

23. A good general rule to follow in filing is that materials should be   23._____

    A. placed in folders quickly
    B. neatly stored
    C. readily available
    D. cross-indexed

24. Items that are filed should be available to   24._____

    A. the secretary charged with the task of filing
    B. secretaries and supervisors
    C. school personnel
    D. the principal

25. A modicum of common sense means _____ common sense. 25._____

    A. an average amount of   B. a great deal of
    C. a little   D. no

———

KEY (CORRECT ANSWERS)

1.	B		11.	D
2.	A		12.	C
3.	C		13.	A
4.	C		14.	A
5.	D		15.	B
6.	B		16.	C
7.	B		17.	C
8.	C		18.	B
9.	A		19.	D
10.	B		20.	B

21.	D
22.	A
23.	C
24.	B
25.	C

———

TEST 3

Questions 1-4.

DIRECTIONS: Questions 1 through 4 are to be answered SOLELY on the basis of the following passage.

The proposition that administrative activity is essentially the same in all organizations appears to underlie some of the practices in the administration of private higher education. Although the practice is unusual in public education, there are numerous instances of industrial, governmental, or military administrators being assigned to private institutions of higher education and, to a lesser extent, of college and university presidents assuming administrative positions in other types of organizations. To test this theory that administrators are interchangeable, there is a need for systematic observation and classification. The myth that an educational administrator must first have experience in the teaching profession is firmly rooted in a long tradition that has historical prestige. The myth is bound up in the expectations of the public and personnel surrounding the administrator. Since administrative success depends significantly on how well an administrator meets the expectations others have of him, the myth may be more powerful than the special experience in helping the administrator attain organizational and educational objectives. Educational administrators who have risen through the teaching profession have often expressed nostalgia for the life of a teacher or scholar, but there is no evidence that this nostalgia contributes to administrative success

1. Which of the following statements as completed is MOST consistent with the above passage? The greatest number of administrators has moved from

    A. industry and the military to government and universities
    B. government and universities to industry and the military
    C. government, the armed forces, and industry to colleges and universities
    D. colleges and universities to government, the armed forces, and industry

2. Of the following, the MOST reasonable inference from the above passage is that a specific area requiring further research is the

    A. place of myth in the tradition and history of the educational profession
    B. relative effectiveness of educational administrators from inside and outside the teaching profession
    C. performance of administrators in the administration of public colleges
    D. degree of reality behind the nostalgia for scholarly pursuits often expressed by educational administrators

3. According to the above passage, the value to an educational administrator of experience in the teaching profession

    A. lies in the firsthand knowledge he has acquired of immediate educational problems
    B. may lie in the belief of his colleagues, subordinates, and the public that such experience is necessary
    C. has been supported by evidence that the experience contributes to administrative success in educational fields
    D. would be greater if the administrator were able to free himself from nostalgia for his former duties

1.____

2.____

3.____

4. Of the following, the MOST suitable title for the above passage is   4._____

    A. EDUCATIONAL ADMINISTRATION, ITS PROBLEMS
    B. THE EXPERIENCE NEEDED FOR EDUCATIONAL ADMINISTRATION
    C. ADMINISTRATION IN HIGHER EDUCATION
    D. EVALUATING ADMINISTRATIVE EXPERIENCE

Questions 5-6.

DIRECTIONS: Questions 5 and 6 are to be answered SOLELY on the basis of the following passage.

    Management by objectives (MBO) may be defined as the process by which the superior and the subordinate managers of an organization jointly define its common goals, define each individual's major areas of responsibility in terms of the results expected of him and use these measures as guides for operating the unit and assessing the contribution of each of its members.

    The MBO approach requires that after organizational goals are established and communicated, targets must be set for each individual position which are congruent with organizational goals. Periodic performance reviews and a final review using the objectives set as criteria are also basic to this approach.

    Recent studies have shown that MBO programs are influenced by attitudes and perceptions of the boss, the company, the reward-punishment system, and the program itself. In addition, the manner in which the MBO program is carried out can influence the success of the program. A study done in the late sixties indicates that the best results are obtained when the manager sets goals which deal with significant problem areas in the organizational unit, or with the subordinate's personal deficiencies. These goals must be clear with regard to what is expected of the subordinate. The frequency of feedback is also important in the success of a management-by-objectives program. Generally, the greater the amount of feedback, the more successful the MBO program.

5. According to the above passage, the expected output for individual employees should be determined   5._____

    A. after a number of reviews of work performance
    B. after common organizational goals are defined
    C. before common organizational goals are defined
    D. on the basis of an employee's personal qualities

6. According to the above passage, the management-by-objectives approach requires   6._____

    A. less feedback than other types of management programs
    B. little review of on-the-job performance after the initial setting of goals
    C. general conformance between individual goals and organizational goals
    D. the setting of goals which deal with minor problem areas in the organization

Questions 7-10.

DIRECTIONS: Questions 7 through 10 are to be answered SOLELY on the basis of the following passage.

Management, which is the function of executive leadership, has as its principal phases the planning, organizing, and controlling of the activities of subordinate groups in the accomplishment of organizational objectives. Planning specifies the kind and extent of the factors, forces, and effects, and the relationships among them, that will be required for satisfactory accomplishment. The nature of the objectives and their requirements must be known before determinations can be made as to what must be done, how it must be done and why, where actions should take place, who should be responsible, and similar problems pertaining to the formulation of a plan. Organizing, which creates the conditions that must be present before the execution of the plan can be undertaken successfully, cannot be done intelligently without knowledge of the organizational objectives. Control, which has to do with the constraint and regulation of activities entering into the execution of the plan, must be exercised in accordance with the characteristics and requirements of the activities demanded by the plan.

7. The one of the following which is the MOST suitable title for the above passage is   7.____

   A. THE NATURE OF SUCCESSFUL ORGANIZATION
   B. THE PLANNING OF MANAGEMENT FUNCTIONS
   C. THE IMPORTANCE OF ORGANIZATIONAL FUNCTIONS
   D. THE PRINCIPLE ASPECTS OF MANAGEMENT

8. It can be inferred from the above passage that the one of the following functions whose   8.____
   existence is essential to the existence of the other three is the

   A. regulation of the work needed to carry out a plan
   B. understanding of what the organization intends to accomplish
   C. securing of information of the factors necessary for accomplishment of objectives
   D. establishment of the conditions required for successful action

9. The one of the following which would NOT be included within any of the principal phases   9.____
   of the function of executive leadership as defined in the above passage is

   A. determination of manpower requirements
   B. procurement of required material
   C. establishment of organizational objectives
   D. scheduling of production

10. The conclusion which can MOST reasonably be drawn from the above passage is that   10.____
    the control phase of managing is most directly concerned with the

    A. influencing of policy determinations
    B. administering of suggestion systems
    C. acquisition of staff for the organization
    D. implementation of performance standards

Questions 11-12.

DIRECTIONS: Questions 11 and 12 are to be answered SOLELY on the basis of the following passage.

Under an open-and-above-board policy, it is to be expected that some supervisors will gloss over known shortcomings of subordinates rather than face the task of discussing them face-to-face. It is also to be expected that at least some employees whose job performance is below par will reject the supervisor's appraisal as biased and unfair. Be that as it may, these are inescapable aspects of any performance appraisal system in which human beings are involved. The supervisor who shies away from calling a spade a spade, as well as the employee with a chip on his shoulder, will each in his own way eventually be revealed in his true light--to the benefit of the organization as a whole.

11. The BEST of the following interpretations of the above passage is that   11.____

   A. the method of rating employee performance requires immediate revision to improve employee acceptance
   B. substandard performance ratings should be discussed with employees even if satisfactory ratings are not
   C. supervisors run the risk of being called unfair by their subordinates even though their appraisals are accurate
   D. any system of employee performance rating is satisfactory if used properly

12. The BEST of the following interpretations of the above passage is that   12.____

   A. supervisors generally are not open-and-above-board with their subordinates
   B. it is necessary for supervisors to tell employees objectively how they are performing
   C. employees complain when their supervisor does not keep them informed
   D. supervisors are afraid to tell subordinates their weaknesses

Questions 13-15.

DIRECTIONS: Questions 13 through 15 are to be answered SOLELY on the basis of the following passage.

During the last decade, a great deal of interest has been generated around the phenomenon of *organizational development,* or the process of developing human resources through conscious organization effort. Organizational development (OD) stresses improving interpersonal relationships and organizational skills, such as communication, to a much greater degree than individual training ever did. The kind of training that an organization should emphasize depends upon the present and future structure of the organization. If future organizations are to be unstable, shifting coalitions, then individual skills and abilities, particularly those emphasizing innovativeness, creativity, flexibility, and the latest technological knowledge, are crucial and individual training is most appropriate.

But if there is to be little change in organizational structure, then the main thrust of training should be group-oriented or organizational development. This approach seems better designed for overcoming hierarchical barriers, for developing a degree of interpersonal relationships which make communication along the chain of command possible, and for retaining a modicum of innovation and/or flexibility.

13. According to the above passage, group-oriented training is MOST useful in   13.____

   A. developing a communications system that will facilitate understanding through the chain of command
   B. highly flexible and mobile organizations
   C. preventing the crossing of hierarchical barriers within an organization
   D. saving energy otherwise wasted on developing methods of dealing with rigid hierarchies

14. The one of the following conclusions which can be drawn MOST appropriately from the   14.____
above passage is that

    A. behavioral research supports the use of organizational development training methods rather than individualized training
    B. it is easier to provide individualized training in specific skills than to set up sensitivity training programs
    C. organizational development eliminates innovative or flexible activity
    D. the nature of an organization greatly influences which training methods will be most effective

15. According to the above passage, the one of the following which is LEAST important for   15.____
large-scale organizations geared to rapid and abrupt change is

    A. current technological information
    B. development of a high degree of interpersonal relationships
    C. development of individual skills and abilities
    D. emphasis on creativity

Questions 16-18.

DIRECTIONS: Questions 16 through 18 are to be answered SOLELY on the basis of the following passage.

The increase in the extent to which each individual is personally responsible to others is most noticeable in a large bureaucracy. No one person *decides* anything; each decision of any importance, is the product of an intricate process of brokerage involving individuals inside and outside the organization who feel some reason to be affected by the decision, or who have special knowledge to contribute to it. The more varied the organization's constituency, the more outside *veto-groups* will need to be taken into account. But even if no outside consultations were involved, sheer size would produce a complex process of decision. For a large organization is a deliberately created system of tensions into which each individual is expected to bring work-ways, viewpoints, and outside relationships markedly different from those of his colleagues. It is the administrator's task to draw from these disparate forces the elements of wise action from day to day, consistent with the purposes of the organization as a whole.

16. The above passage is essentially a description of decision making as   16.____

    A. an organization process
    B. the key responsibility of the administrator
    C. the one best position among many
    D. a complex of individual decisions

17. Which one of the following statements BEST describes the responsibilities of an administrator?   17.____

    A. He modifies decisions and goals in accordance with pressures from within and outside the organization.
    B. He creates problem-solving mechanisms that rely on the varied interests of his staff and *veto-groups*.
    C. He makes determinations that will lead to attainment of his agency's objectives.
    D. He obtains agreement among varying viewpoints and interests.

18. In the context of the operations of a central public personnel agency, a *veto group* would
LEAST likely consist of

    A. employee organizations
    B. professional personnel societies
    C. using agencies
    D. civil service newspapers

18.____

Questions 19-25.

DIRECTIONS: Questions 19 through 25 are to be answered SOLELY on the basis of the following passage, which is an extract from a report prepared for Department X, which outlines the procedure to be followed in the case of transfers of employees.

Every transfer, regardless of the reason therefore, requires completion of the record of transfer, Form DT 411. To denote consent to the transfer, DT 411 should contain the signatures of the transferee and the personnel officer(s) concerned, except that, in the case of an involuntary transfer, the signatures of the transferee's present and prospective supervisors shall be entered in Boxes 8A and 8B, respectively, since the transferee does not consent. Only a permanent employee may request a transfer; in such cases, the employee's attendance record shall be duly considered with regard to absences, latenesses, and accrued overtime balances. In the case of an inter-district transfer, the employee's attendance record must be included in Section 8A of the transfer request, Form DT 410, by the personnel officer of the district from which the transfer is requested. The personnel officer of the district to which the employee requested transfer may refuse to accept accrued overtime balances in excess of ten days.

An employee on probation shall be eligible for transfer. If such employee is involuntarily transferred, he shall be credited for the period of time already served on probation. However, if such transfer is voluntary, the employee shall be required to serve the entire period of his probation in the new position. An employee who has occurred a disability which prevents him from performing his normal duties may be transferred during the period of such disability to other appropriate duties. A disability transfer requires the completion of either Form DT 414 if the disability is job-connected, or Form DT 415 if it is not a job-connected disability. In either case, the personnel officer of the district from which the transfer is made signs in Box 6A of the first two copies and the personnel officer of the district to which the transfer is made signs in Box 6B of the last two copies, or, in the case of an intra-district disability transfer, the personnel officer must sign in Box 6A of the first two copies and Box 6B of the last two copies.

19. When a personnel officer consents to an employee's request for transfer from his district,
this procedure requires that the personnel officer sign Form(s)

    A. DT 411
    B. DT 410 and DT 411
    C. DT 411 and either Form DT 414 or DT 415
    D. DT 410 and DT 411, and either Form DT 414 or DT 415

19.___

20. With respect to the time record of an employee transferred against his wishes during his
probationary period, this procedure requires that

    A. he serve the entire period of his probation in his present office
    B. he lose his accrued overtime balance

20.___

C.   his attendance record be considered with regard to absences and latenesses

D.   he be given credit for the period of time he has already served on probation

21.   Assume you are a supervisor and an employee must be transferred into your office against his wishes. According to the this procedure, the box you must sign on the record of transfer is   21._____

    A. 6A   B. 8A   C. 6B   D. 8B

22.   Under this procedure, in the case of a disability transfer, when must Box 6A on Forms DT 414 and DT 415 be signed by the personnel officer of the district to which the transfer is being made?   22._____

    A.   In all cases when either Form DT 414 or Form DT 415 is used

    B.   In all cases when Form DT 414 is used and only under certain circumstances when Form DT 415 is used

    C.   In all cases when Form DT 415 is used and only under certain circumstances when Form DT 414 is used

    D.   Only under certain circumstances when either Form DT 414 or Form DT 415 is used

23.   From the above passage, it may be inferred MOST correctly that the number of copies of Form DT 414 is   23._____

    A.   no more than 2

    B.   at least 3

    C.   at least 5

    D.   more than the number of copies of Form DT 415

24.   A change in punctuation and capitalization only which would change one sentence into two and possibly contribute to somewhat greater ease of reading this report extract would be MOST appropriate in the   24._____

    A.   2nd sentence, 1st paragraph

    B.   3rd sentence, 1st paragraph

    C.   next to he last sentence, 2nd paragraph

    D.   2nd sentence, 2nd paragraph

25.   In the second paragraph, a word that is INCORRECTLY used is   25._____

    A.   *shall* in the 1st sentence

    B.   *voluntary* in the 3rd sentence

    C.   *occurred* in the 4th sentence

    D.   *intra-district* in the last sentence

KEY (CORRECT ANSWERS)

1. C
2. B
3. B
4. B
5. B

6. C
7. D
8. B
9. C
10. D

11. C
12. B
13. A
14. D
15. B

16. A
17. C
18. B
19. A
20. D

21. D
22. D
23. B
24. B
25. C

DOCUMENTS AND FORMS
PREPARING WRITTEN MATERIAL
EXAMINATION SECTION

TEST 1

DIRECTIONS: Each question or incomplete statement is followed by several suggested answers or completions. Select the one that BEST answers the question or completes the statement. *PRINT THE LETTER OF THE CORRECT ANSWER IN THE SPACE AT THE RIGHT.*

1. Suppose that one of the forms you fill out daily requires some information which you know is unnecessary.
   Which is the BEST action to take?
   A. Refuse to supply the information you think is unnecessary.
   B. Continue to fill out the form as required, even though the information is unnecessary.
   C. Suggest to your supervisor that the form be revised to reflect useful information.
   D. Suggest that fewer copies of the form be required.

1.____

2. Of the following, the MOST likely reason for recommending that your department establish a standard form for recording certain information would be that this information
   A. will be produced at some disciplinary hearing
   B. concerns a secret or confidential record about an unusual incident at the garage
   C. contains a detailed explanation of a complex procedure
   D. must be taken from a large number of people on a regular basis

2.____

3. If the four steps listed below for processing records were given in logical sequence, the one that would be the THIRD step is
   A. coding the records, using a chart or classification system
   B. inspecting the records to make sure they have been released for filing
   C. preparing cross-reference sheets or cards
   D. skimming the records to determine filing captions

3.____

4. Which of the following BEST describes "office work simplification"?
   A. An attempt to increase the rate of production by speeding up the movements of employees
   B. Eliminating wasteful steps in order to increase efficiency
   C. Making jobs as easy as possible for employees so they will not be overworked
   D. Eliminating all difficult tasks from an office and leaving only simple ones

4.____

5. The use of the same method of recordkeeping and reporting by all sections is   5.____
    A. *desirable*, mainly because it saves time in section operations
    B. *undesirable*, mainly because it kills the initiative of the individual section foreman
    C. *desirable*, mainly because it will be easier for the superior to evaluate and compare section operations
    D. *undesirable*, mainly because operations vary from section to section and uniform recordkeeping and reporting is not appropriate

6. The GREATEST benefit the section officer will have from keeping complete   6.____
    and accurate records of section operations is that
    A. he will find it easier to run his section efficiently
    B. he will need less equipment
    C. he will need less manpower
    D. the section will run smoothly when he is out

7. You have prepared a report to your superior and are ready to send it forward.   7.____
    But on reading it, you think some parts are not clearly expressed and the
    superior may have difficulty getting your point.
    Of the following, it would be BEST for you to
    A. give the report to one of your men to read, and, if he has no trouble understanding it, send it through
    B. forward the report and call the superior the next day to ask if it was all right
    C. forward the report as is; higher echelons should be able to understand any report prepared by a section officer
    D. do the report over, re-writing the sections you are doubtful of

8. Of the following, a flow chart is BEST described as a chart which shows   8.____
    A. the places through which work moves in the course of the job process
    B. which employees perform specific functions leading to the completion of a job
    C. the schedules for production and how they eliminate waiting time between jobs
    D. how work units are affected by the actions of related work units

9. A superior decided to hold a problem-solving conference with his entire staff   9.____
    and distributed an announcement and agenda one week before the meeting.
    Of the following, the BEST reason for providing each participate with an
    agenda is that
    A. participants will feel that something will be accomplished
    B. participants may prepare for the conference
    C. controversy will be reduced
    D. the top man should state the expected conclusions

10. The one of the following activities which is generally the LEAST proper   10.____
function of a centralized procedures section is
   A. issuing new and revised procedural instructions
   B. coordinating forms revision and procedural changes
   C. accepting or rejecting authorized procedural changes
   D. controlling standard numbering systems for procedural releases

11. Assume that it is the policy of an operating unit to act on all requests   11.____
received within five working days. Several operations are involved in acting on
these requests. Each operation is performed by a separate sub-unit. The staff
of the unit is reasonable adequate to handle this workload.
If only one of the following can be done, the MOST effective procedure for
maintaining adherence to the unit's five-day processing policy is to
   A. maintain a central "tickler" file in each sub-unit for the requests received
      daily in that sub-unit
   B. prepare a "tickler" card for each request and follow it up five days later to
      determine whether action has been taken
   C. rely on standards of production for each operation as an incentive to the
      employees of each sub-unit to meet the schedule
   D. schedule the operations on a timetable basis so that the request will be
      forwarded from one sub-unit to another within specified time limits

12. When one or two simple changes are needed in a memo to another unit or   12.____
in a letter to a citizen, a unit head follows the practice of making such simple
changes neatly in ink.
This practice is GENERALLY
   A. *poor*, chiefly because it reflects unfavorably on the originating unit's ability
      to make a decision
   B. *good*, chiefly because the department's public image is likely to be
      improved when people see it as trying to save money and speed up its
      processes
   C. *poor*, chiefly because a letter or document prepared in final form
      represents an investment of department time and effort and should go out
      only as a perfect finished product
   D. *good*, chiefly because the document may be important, and sending it
      back for retyping may delay it too long to achieve its purpose

13. Suppose that one of the office machines in your unit is badly in need of   13.____
replacement.
Of the following, the MOST important reason for postponing immediate
purchase of a new machine would be that
   A. a later model of the machine is expected on the market in a few months
   B. the new machine is more expensive than the old machine
   C. the operator of the present machine will have to be instructed by the
      manufacturer in the operation of the new machine
   D. the employee operating the old machine is not complaining

14. To avoid cutting off parts of letters when using an automatic letter opener, it is BEST to
    A. arrange all of the letters so that the addresses are right side up
    B. hold the envelopes up to the light to make sure their contents have not settled to the side that is to be opened
    C. strike the envelopes against a table or desktop several times so that the contents of all the envelopes settle to one side
    D. check the enclosures periodically to make sure that the machine has not been cutting into them

14.____

15. Of the following, the BEST reason for setting up a partitioned work area for the typists in our office is that
    A. an uninterrupted flow of work among the typists will be possible
    B. complaints about ventilation and lighting will be reduced
    C. the first-line supervisor will have more direct control over the typists
    D. the noise of the typewriters will be less disturbing to other workers

15.____

16. From the viewpoint of use of a typewriter to fill in a form, the MOST important design factor to consider is
    A. standard spacing   B. box headings
    C. serial numbering   D. vertical guide lines

16.____

17. Requests to repair office equipment which appears to be unsafe should be given priority MAINLY because, if repairs are delayed,
    A. there may be injuries to staff
    B. there may be further deterioration of the equipment
    C. work flow may be interrupted
    D. the cost of repair may increase

17.____

18. A clerk is asked to complete two assignments – transcribe a handwritten business letter and create a spreadsheet. Which two computer programs would the clerk use?
    A. Microsoft Word and Microsoft Excel
    B. Microsoft Word and Microsoft PowerPoint
    C. Google Docs and Google Chrome
    D. Adobe Reader and Microsoft PowerPoint

18.____

19. Generally, the actual floor space occupied by a standard letter-size office file cabinet, when closed, is MOST NEARLY
    A. ½ square foot   B. 3 square feet
    C. 7 square feet   D. 11 square feet

19.____

20. Suppose a clerk under your supervision accidentally opens a personal letter while handling office mail.
Under such circumstances, you should tell the clerk to put the letter back into the envelope and
    A. take the letter to the person to whom it belongs and make sure he understands that the clerk did not read it
    B. try to seal the envelope so it won't appear to have been opened

20.____

C. write on the envelope "Sorry – opened by mistake," and put his initials on it
D. write on the envelope "Sorry – opened by mistake," but not put his initials on it

21. Standard forms frequently call for entries on them to be printed.
     The MAIN reason for this practice is that printing, as compared to writing, is
     GENERALLY
     A. more compact   B. more legal
     C. more legible   D. easier to do

21.____

22. After a stenographer types a letter which has been dictated, the finished
     letter should be carefully read for errors.
     If he dictator follows the procedure of carefully reading each transcribed letter,
     a stenographer, under your supervision, should, unless you instruct her
     otherwise
     A. not take time to proofread transcribed letters
     B. continue to carefully proofread transcribed letters
     C. review transcribed letters for meaning rather than for errors in typing or
         transcription
     D. review transcribed letters for errors in typing rather than for errors in
         transcription

22.____

23. In transcribing a letter, the secretary notes that the dictator said, "The series
     of conferences are planned to be relevant to today's problems." In such a
     case, the secretary should
     A. type the sentence as it appears in the notes
     B. check with the dictator to see whether he would prefer a different
         grammatical construction
     C. change the noun so that it is correct
     D. revise the sentence as much as necessary to make it read better

23.____

24. Of the following, the BEST procedure for your staff to follow in transcribing
     several letters that were dictated is to
     A. transcribe first the letters that are most difficult so that they can return
         immediately to the dictator with any questions
     B. read through the notes for each letter to be sure they have all the
         information needed before preparing the transcript
     C. transcribe first those letters that are shortest and simplest in order to get
         them out of the way
     D. read all the notes aloud to a co-worker to see whether they sound right

24.____

25. In typing long letters, which of the following is generally considered the
     LEAST desirable practice?
     A. Numbering the second and succeeding pages of the letter
     B. Typing a single line of a new paragraph as the last line of a page
     C. Dividing a word at the end of a line of typing
     D. Typing the name of the recipient of the letter on the second and
         succeeding pages

25.____

KEY (CORRECT ANSWERS)

1.	C		11.	D
2.	D		12.	B
3.	D		13.	A
4.	B		14.	C
5.	C		15.	D
6.	A		16.	A
7.	D		17.	A
8.	A		18.	A
9.	B		19.	B
10.	C		20.	C

21.	C
22.	B
23.	B
24.	B
25.	B

TEST 2

DIRECTIONS: Each question or incomplete statement is followed by several suggested answers or completions. Select the one that BEST answers the question or completes the statement. *PRINT THE LETTER OF THE CORRECT ANSWER IN THE SPACE AT THE RIGHT.*

1. The use of a microfilm system for information storage and retrieval would make the MOST sense in an office where
   A. a great number of documents must be kept available for permanent reference
   B. documents are ordinarily kept on file for less than six months
   C. filing is a minor and unimportant part of the office work
   D. most of the records on file are working forms on which additional entries are frequently made

   1.____

2. Of the following concepts, the one which CANNOT be represented suitably by a pie chart is
   A. percent shares
   B. shares in absolute units
   C. time trends
   D. successive totals over time, with their shares

   2.____

3. A pictogram is ESSENTIALLY another version of a(n) _____ chart.
   A. plain bar
   B. component bar
   C. pie
   D. area

   3.____

4. A time series for a certain cost is presented in a graph. It is drawn so that the vertical (cost) axis starts at a point well above zero. This is a legitimate method of presentation for some purposes, but it may have the effect of
   A. hiding fixed components of the cost
   B. exaggerating changes which, in actual amounts, may be insignificant
   C. minimizing variable components of the cost
   D. impairing correlation analysis

   4.____

5. Certain budgetary data may be represented by bar, area, or volume charts. Which one of the following BEST expressed the most appropriate order of usefulness?
   A. Descends from bar to volume and area charts, the last two being about the same
   B. Descends from volume to area, to bar charts
   C. Depends on the nature of the data presented
   D. Descends from bar to area to volume charts

   5.____

6. One weekend, you develop a painful infection in one hand. You know that   6.____
   your typing speed will be much slower than normal and the likelihood of your
   making mistakes will be increased.
   Of the following, the BEST course of action for you to take in this situation is to
   A. report to work as scheduled and do your typing assignments as best you
      can without complaining
   B. report to work as scheduled and ask your co-workers to divide your typing
      assignments until your hand heals
   C. report to work as scheduled and ask your supervisor for non-typing
      assignments until your hand heals
   D. call in sick and remain on medical leave until your hand is completely
      healed so that you can perform your normal duties

7. When filling out a departmental form during an interview concerning a citizen   7.____
   complaint, an interviewer should know the purpose of each question that he
   asks the citizen. For such information to be supplied by your department is
   A. *advisable*, because the interviewer may lose interest in the job if he is not
      fully informed about the questions he has to ask
   B. *inadvisable*, because the interviewer may reveal the true purpose of the
      questions to the citizens
   C. *advisable*, because the interviewer might otherwise record superficial or
      inadequate answers if he does not fully understand the questions
   D. *inadvisable*, because the information obtained through the form may be of
      little importance to the interviewer

8. The one of the following which is the BEST reason for placing the date and   8.____
   time of receipt on incoming mail is that this procedure
   A. aids the filing of correspondence in alphabetical order
   B. fixes responsibility for promptness in answering correspondence
   C. indicates that the mail has been checked for the presence of a return
      address
   D. makes it easier to distribute the main in sequence

9. Which one of the following is the FIRST step that you should take when filing   9.____
   a document by subject?
   A. Arrange related documents by date with the latest date in front
   B. Check whether the document has been released for filing
   C. Cross-reference the document if necessary
   D. Determine the category under which the document will be filed

10. The one of the following which is NOT generally employed to keep track of   10.____
    frequently used material requiring future attention is a
    A. card tickler file   B. dated follow-up folder
    C. periodic transferal of records   D. signal folder

11. Which one of the following is NOT a useful filing practice?   11.____
    A. Filing active records in the most accessible parts of the file cabinet
    B. Filing a file drawer to capacity in order to save space
    C. Gluing small documents to standard-size paper before filing
    D. Using different colored labels for various filing categories

12. The one of the following cases in which you would NOT place a special   12.____
notation in the left margin of a letter that you have typed is when
    A. one of the copies is intended for someone other than the addressee of
       the letter
    B. you enclose a flyer with the letter
    C. you sign your superior's name to the letter, at his or her request
    D. the letter refers to something being sent under separate cover

13. Suppose that you accidentally cut a letter or enclosure as you are opening   13.____
an envelope with a paper knife. The one of the following that you should do
FIRST is to
    A. determine whether the document is important
    B. clip or staple the pieces together and process as usual
    C. mend the cut document with transparent tape
    D. notify the sender that the communication was damaged and request
       another copy

14. It is generally advisable to leave at least six inches of working space in a   14.____
file drawer. This procedure is MOST useful in
    A. decreasing the number of filing errors
    B. facilitating the sorting of documents and folders
    C. maintaining a regular program of removing inactive records
    D. preventing folders and papers from being torn

15. Of the following, the MOST important reason to sort large volumes of   15.____
documents before filing is that sorting
    A. decreases the need for cross-referencing
    B. eliminates the need to keep the filing up-to-date
    C. prevents overcrowding of the file drawers
    D. saves time and energy in filing

16. When typing a preliminary draft of a report, the one of the following which   16.____
you should generally NOT do is to
    A. erase typing errors and deletions rather than "X"ing them out
    B. leave plenty of room at the top, bottom, and sides of each page
    C. make only the number of copies that you are asked to make
    D. type double or triple space

17. When printing a 500-page office manual, the most efficient method is to use   17.____
which of the following office machines?
    A. Inkjet printer
    B. Copy machine
    C. Word processor
    D. All-in-one scanner/fax/copier

18. When typing name or titles on a roll of folder labels, the one of the following   18.____
which it is MOST important to do is to type the caption
    A. as it appears son the papers to be placed in the folder
    B. in capital letters
    C. in exact indexing or filing order
    D. so that it appears near the bottom of the folder tab when the label is
      attached

19. The MOST important reason for having color cartridges on hand for an office copier   19.____
even though most prints are black and white is because
    A. color ink is used for all copies
    B. some copiers or printers will not print black and white if any of the color
      cartridges are empty
    C. black ink is cheaper when purchasing along with color cartridges
    D. lack of color ink can cause copier malfunctions

20. All of the following pertain to the formatting of word-processing documents EXCEPT   20.____
    A. headers and footers
    B. rows and columns
    C. indents and page breaks
    D. alignment and justified type

KEY (CORRECT ANSWERS)

1.	A	11.	B
2.	C	12.	C
3.	A	13.	C
4.	B	14.	D
5.	D	15.	D
6.	C	16.	A
7.	C	17.	B
8.	B	18.	C
9.	B	19.	B
10.	C	20.	B

PREPARING WRITTEN MATERIALS

EXAMINATION SECTION
TEST 1

DIRECTIONS: Each question consists of a sentence which may be classified appropriately under one of the following four categories:

A. Incorrect because of faulty grammar or sentence structure;
B. Incorrect because of faulty punctuation;
C. Incorrect because of faulty capitalization;
D. Correct.

Examine each sentence carefully. Then, in the space at the right, indicate the letter preceding the category which is the BEST of the four suggested above. Each incorrect sentence contains only one type of error. Consider a sentence correct if it contains no errors, although there may be other correct ways of expressing the same thought.

1. All the employees, in this office, are over twenty-one years old.   1._____

2. Neither the clerk nor the stenographer was able to explain what had happened.   2._____

3. Mr. Johnson did not know who he would assign to type the order.   3._____

4. Mr. Marshall called her to report for work on Saturday.   4._____

5. He might of arrived on time if the train had not been delayed.   5._____

6. Some employees on the other hand, are required to fill out these forms every month.   6._____

7. The supervisor issued special instructions to his subordinates to prevent their making errors.   7._____

8. Our supervisor Mr. Williams, expects to be promoted in about two weeks.   8._____

9. We were informed that prof. Morgan would attend the conference.   9._____

10. The clerks were assigned to the old building; the stenographers, to the new building.   10._____

11. The supervisor asked Mr. Smith and I to complete the work as quickly as possible.   11._____

12. He said, that before an employee can be permitted to leave, the report must be finished.   12._____

13. An adding machine, in addition to the three typewriters, are needed in the new office.   13._____

14. Having made many errors in her work, the supervisor asked the typist to be more careful.   14._____

15. "If you are given an assignment," he said, "you should begin work on it as quickly as possible."   15._____

16. All the clerks, including those who have been appointed recently are required to work on the new assignment.   16._____

17. The office manager asked each employee to work one Saturday a month.   17.____

18. Neither Mr. Smith nor Mr. Jones was able to finish his assignment on time.   18.____

19. The task of filing these cards is to be divided equally between you and he.   19.____

20. He is an employee whom we consider to be efficient.   20.____

21. I believe that the new employees are not as punctual as us.   21.____

22. The employees, working in this office, are to be congratulated for their work.   22.____

23. The delay in preparing the report was caused, in his opinion, by the lack of proper super-vision and coordination.   23.____

24. John Jones accidentally pushed the wrong button and then all the lights went out.   24.____

25. The investigator ought to of had the witness sign the statement.   25.____

KEY (CORRECT ANSWERS)

1.	B		11.	A
2.	D		12.	B
3.	A		13.	A
4.	C		14.	A
5.	A		15.	D
6.	B		16.	B
7.	D		17.	C
8.	B		18.	D
9.	C		19.	A
10.	D		20.	D

21.	A
22.	B
23.	D
24.	D
25.	A

TEST 2

Questions 1-10.

DIRECTIONS: Each of the following sentences may be classified under one of the following four options:
- A. Faulty; contains an error in grammar only
- B. Faulty; contains an error in spelling only
- C. Faulty; contains an error in grammar and an error in spelling
- D. Correct; contains no error in grammar or in spelling

Examine each sentence carefully to determine under which of the above four options it is BEST classified. Then, in the space at the right, write the letter preceding the option which is the best of the four listed above.

1. A recognized principle of good management is that an assignment should be given to whomever is best qualified to carry it out. 1._____

2. He considered it a privilege to be allowed to review and summarize the technical reports issued annually by your agency. 2._____

3. Because the warehouse was in an inaccessable location, deliveries of electric fixtures from the warehouse were made only in large lots. 3._____

4. Having requisitioned the office supplies, Miss Brown returned to her desk and resumed the computation of petty cash disbursements. 4._____

5. One of the advantages of this chemical solution is that records treated with it are not inflamable. 5._____

6. The complaint of this employee, in addition to the complaints of the other employees, were submitted to the grievance committee. 6._____

7. A study of the duties and responsibilities of each of the various categories of employees was conducted by an unprejudiced classification analyst. 7._____

8. Ties of friendship with this subordinate compels him to withold the censure that the subordinate deserves. 8._____

9. Neither of the agencies are affected by the decision to institute a program for rehabilitating physically handi-caped men and women. 9._____

10. The chairman stated that the argument between you and he was creating an intolerable situation. 10._____

Questions 11-25.

DIRECTIONS: Each of the following sentences may be classified under one of the following four options:

A. Correct
B. Sentence contains an error in spelling
C. Sentence contains an error in grammar
D. Sentence contains errors in both grammar and spelling.

11. He reported that he had had a really good time during his vacation although the farm was located in a very inaccessible portion of the country.   11._____

12. It looks to me like he has been fasinated by that beautiful painting.   12._____

13. We have permitted these kind of pencils to accumulate on our shelves, knowing we can sell them at a profit of five cents apiece any time we choose.   13._____

14. Believing that you will want an unexaggerated estimate of the amount of business we can expect, I have made every effort to secure accurate figures.   14._____

15. Each and every man, woman and child in that untrameled wilderness carry guns for protection against the wild animals.   15._____

16. Although this process is different than the one to which he is accustomed, a good chemist will have no trouble.   16._____

17. Insensible to the fuming and fretting going on about him, the engineer continued to drive the mammoth dynamo to its utmost capacity.   17._____

18. Everyone had studied his lesson carefully and was consequently well prepared when the instructor began to discuss the fourth dimention.   18._____

19. I learned Johnny six new arithmetic problems this afternoon.   19._____

20. Athletics is urged by our most prominent citizens as the pursuit which will enable the younger generation to achieve that ideal of education, a sound mind in a sound body.   20._____

21. He did not see whoever was at the door very clearly but thinks it was the city tax appraiser.   21._____

22. He could not scarsely believe that his theories had been substantiated in this convincing fashion.   22._____

23. Although you have displayed great ingenuity in carrying out your assignments, the choice for the position still lies among Brown and Smith.   23._____

24. If they had have pleaded at the time that Smith was an accessory to the crime, it would have lessened the punishment.   24._____

25. It has proven indispensible in his compilation of the facts in the matter.   25._____

KEY (CORRECT ANSWERS)

1.	A		11.	A
2.	D		12.	D
3.	B		13.	C
4.	D		14.	B
5.	B		15.	D
6.	A		16.	C
7.	D		17.	A
8.	C		18.	B
9.	C		19.	C
10.	A		20.	A

21.	B
22.	D
23.	C
24.	D
25.	B

TEST 3

Questions 1-5.

DIRECTIONS: Questions 1 through 5 consist of sentences which may or may not contain errors in grammar or spelling or both. Sentences which do not contain errors in grammar or spelling or both are to be considered correct, even though there may be other correct ways of expressing the same thought. Examine each sentence carefully. Then, in the space at the right, write the letter of the answer which is the BEST of those suggested below:
   A. If the sentence is correct;
   B. If the sentence contains an error in spelling;
   C. If the sentence contains an error in grammar;
   D. If the sentence contains errors in both grammar and spelling.

1. Brown is doing fine although the work is irrevelant to his training.   1.____

2. The conference of sales managers voted to set its adjournment at one o'clock in order to give those present an opportunity to get rid of all merchandise.   2.____

3. He decided that in view of what had taken place at the hotel that he ought to stay and thank the benificent stranger who had rescued him from an embarassing situation.   3.____

4. Since you object to me criticizing your letter, I have no alternative but to consider you a mercenary scoundrel.   4.____

5. I rushed home ahead of schedule so that you will leave me go to the picnic with Mary.   5.____

Questions 6-15.

DIRECTIONS: Some of the following sentences contain an error in spelling, word usage, or sentence structure, or punctuation. Some sentences are correct as they stand although there may be other correct ways of expressing the same thought. All incorrect sentences contain only one error. Mark your answer to each question in the space at the right as follows:
   A. If the sentence has an error in spelling;
   B. If the sentence has an error in punctuation or capitalization;
   C. If the sentence has an error in word usage or sentence structure;
   D. If the sentence is correct.

6. Because the chairman failed to keep the participants from wandering off into irrelevant discussions, it was impossible to reach a consensus before the meeting was adjourned.   6.____

7. Certain employers have an unwritten rule that any applicant, who is over 55 years of age, is automatically excluded from consideration for any position whatsoever.   7.____

8. If the proposal to build schools in some new apartment buildings were to be accepted by the builders, one of the advantages that could be expected to result would be better communication between teachers and parents of schoolchildren.   8.____

9. In this instance, the manufacturer's violation of the law against deseptive packaging was discernible only to an experienced inspector.   9.____

10. The tenants' anger stemmed from the president's going to Washington to testify without consulting them first.   10.____

11. Did the president of this eminent banking company say; "We intend to hire and train a number of these disadvan-taged youths?"   11.____

12. In addition, today's confidential secretary must be knowledgable in many different areas: for example, she must know modern techniques for making travel arrangements for the executive.   12.____

13. To avoid further disruption of work in the offices, the protesters were forbidden from entering the building unless they had special passes.   13.____

14. A valuable secondary result of our training conferences is the opportunities afforded for management to observe the reactions of the participants.   14.____

15. Of the two proposals submitted by the committee, the first one is the best.   15.____

Questions 16-25.

DIRECTIONS: Each of the following sentences may be classified MOST appropriately under one of the following three categories:
A. Faulty because of incorrect grammar
B. Faulty because of incorrect punctuation
C. Correct

Examine each sentence. Then, print the capital letter preceding the BEST choice of the three suggested above. All incorrect sentences contain only one type of error. Consider a sentence correct if it contains none of the types of errors mentioned, even though there may be other ways of expressing the same thought.

16. He sent the notice to the clerk who you hired yesterday.   16.____

17. It must be admitted, however that you were not informed of this change.   17.____

18. Only the employees who have served in this grade for at least two years are eligible for promotion.   18.____

19. The work was divided equally between she and Mary.   19.____

20. He thought that you were not available at that time.   20.____

21. When the messenger returns; please give him this package.   21.____

22. The new secretary prepared, typed, addressed, and delivered, the notices.   22.____

23. Walking into the room, his desk can be seen at the rear.   23.____

24. Although John has worked here longer than she, he produces a smaller amount of work.   24.____

25. She said she could of typed this report yesterday.   25.____

____

KEY (CORRECT ANSWERS)

1.	D	11.	B
2.	A	12.	A
3.	D	13.	C
4.	C	14.	D
5.	C	15.	C
6.	A	16.	A
7.	B	17.	B
8.	D	18.	C
9.	A	19.	A
10.	D	20.	C

21.	B
22.	B
23.	A
24.	C
25.	A

TEST 4

Questions 1-5.

DIRECTIONS: Each of the following sentences may be classified MOST appropriately under one of the following three categories:
    A. Faulty because of incorrect grammar
    B. Faulty because of incorrect punctuation
    C. Correct

Examine each sentence. Then, print the capital letter preceding the BEST choice of the three suggested above. All incorrect sentences contain only one type of error. Consider a sentence correct if it contains none of the types of errors mentioned, even though there may be other correct ways of expressing the same thought.

1. Neither one of these procedures are adequate for the efficient performance of this task.   1._____

2. The typewriter is the tool of the typist; the cash register, the tool of the cashier.   2._____

3. "The assignment must be completed as soon as possible" said the supervisor.   3._____

4. As you know, office handbooks are issued to all new employees.   4._____

5. Writing a speech is sometimes easier than to deliver it before an audience.   5._____

Questions 6-15.

DIRECTIONS: Each statement given in Questions 6 through 15 contains one of the faults of English usage listed below. For each, choose from the options listed the MAJOR fault contained.
    A. The statement is not a complete sentence.
    B. The statement contains a word or phrase that is redundant.
    C. The statement contains a long, less commonly used word when a shorter, more direct word would be acceptable.
    D. The statement contains a colloquial expression that normally is avoided in business writing.

6. The fact that this activity will afford an opportunity to meet your group.   6._____

7. Do you think that the two groups can join together for next month's meeting?   7._____

8. This is one of the most exciting new innovations to be introduced into our college.   8._____

9. We expect to consummate the agenda before the meeting ends tomorrow at noon.   9._____

10. While this seminar room is small in size, we think we can use it.   10._____

11. Do you think you can make a modification in the date of the Budget Committee meeting?   11._____

12. We are cognizant of the problem but we think we can ameliorate the situation.   12._____

13. Shall I call you around three on the day I arrive in the City?   13._____

14. Until such time that we know precisely that the students will be present.   14._____

15. The consensus of opinion of all the members present is reported in the minutes.   15._____

Questions 16-25.

DIRECTIONS: For each of Questions 16 through 25, select from the options given below the
                        MOST applicable choice.
     A.   The sentence is correct.
     B.   The sentence contains a spelling error only.
     C.   The sentence contains an English grammar error only.
     D.   The sentence contains both a spelling error and an English grammar
        error.

16. Every person in the group is going to do his share.   16._____

17. The man who we selected is new to this University.   17._____

18. She is the older of the four secretaries on the two staffs that are to be combined.   18._____

19. The decision has to be made between him and I.   19._____

20. One of the volunteers are too young for this complecated task, don't you think?   20._____

21. I think your idea is splindid and it will improve this report considerably.   21._____

22. Do you think this is an exagerated account of the behavior you and me observed this   22._____
morning?

23. Our supervisor has a clear idea of excelence.   23._____

24. How many occurences were verified by the observers?   24._____

25. We must complete the typing of the draft of the questionaire by noon tomorrow.   25._____

KEY (CORRECT ANSWERS)

1.	A	11.	C
2.	C	12.	C
3.	B	13.	D
4.	C	14.	A
5.	A	15.	B
6.	A	16.	A
7.	B	17.	C
8.	B	18.	C
9.	C	19.	C
10.	B	20.	D

21.	B
22.	D
23.	B
24.	B
25.	B

PREPARING WRITTEN MATERIAL

PARAGRAPH REARRANGEMENT
COMMENTARY

The sentences which follow are in scrambled order. You are to rearrange them in proper order and indicate the letter choice containing the correct answer at the space at the right.

Each group of sentences in this section is actually a paragraph presented in scrambled order. Each sentence in the group has a place in that paragraph; no sentence is to be left out. You are to read each group of sentences and decide upon the best order in which to put the sentences so as to form as well-organized paragraph.

The questions in this section measure the ability to solve a problem when all the facts relevant to its solution are not given.

More specifically, certain positions of responsibility and authority require the employee to discover connections between events sometimes, apparently, unrelated. In order to do this, the employee will find it necessary to correctly infer that unspecified events have probably occurred or are likely to occur. This ability becomes especially important when action must be taken on incomplete information.

Accordingly, these questions require competitors to choose among several suggested alternatives, each of which presents a different sequential arrangement of the events. Competitors must choose the MOST logical of the suggested sequences.

In order to do so, they may be required to draw on general knowledge to infer missing concepts or events that are essential to sequencing the given events. Competitors should be careful to infer only what is essential to the sequence. The plausibility of the wrong alternatives will always require the inclusion of unlikely events or of additional chains of events which are NOT essential to sequencing the given events.

It's very important to remember that you are looking for the best of the four possible choices, and that the best choice of all may not even be one of the answers you're given to choose from.

There is no one right way to solve these problems. Many people have found it helpful to first write out the order of the sentences, as they would have arranged them, on their scrap paper before looking at the possible answers. If their optimum answer is there, this can save them some time. If it isn't, this method can still give insight into solving the problem. Others find it most helpful to just go through each of the possible choices, contrasting each as they go along. You should use whatever method feels comfortable, and works, for you.

While most of these types of questions are not that difficult, we've added a higher percentage of the difficult type, just to give you more practice. Usually there are only one or two questions on this section that contain such subtle distinctions that you're unable to answer confidently, and you then may find yourself stuck deciding between two possible choices, neither of which you're sure about.

EXAMINATION SECTION
TEST 1

DIRECTIONS: The following groups of sentences need to be arranged in an order that makes sense. Select the letter preceding the sequence that represents the BEST sentence order. *PRINT THE LETTER OF THE CORRECT ANSWER IN THE SPACE AT THE RIGHT.*

1.   I.   The keyboard was purposely designed to be a little awkward to slow typists down.   1.____

      II. The arrangement of letters on the keyboard of a typewriter was not designed for the convenience of the typist.

      III. Fortunately, no one is suggesting that a new keyboard be designed right away.

      IV. If one were, we would have to learn to type all over again.

      V. The reason was that the early machines were slower than the typists and would jam easily.

      A. I, III, IV, II, V   B. II, V, I, IV, III
      C. V, I, II, III, IV   D. II, I, V, III, IV

2.   I.   The majority of the new service jobs are part-time or low-paying.   2.____

      II. According to the U.S. Bureau of Labor Statistics, jobs in the service sector constitute 72% of all jobs in this country.

      III. If more and more workers receive less and less money, who will buy the goods and services needed to keep the economy going?

      IV. The service sector is by far the fastest growing part of the United States economy.

      V. Some economists look upon this trend with great concern.

      A. II, IV, I, V, III   B. II, III, IV, I, V
      C. V, IV, II, III, I   D. III, I, II, IV, V

3.   I.   They can also affect one's endurance.   3.____

      II. This can stabilize blood sugar levels, and ensure that the brain is receiving a steady, constant supply of glucose, so that one is *hitting on all cylinders* while taking the test.

      III. By food, we mean real food, not junk food or unhealthy snacks.

      IV. For this reason, it is important not to skip a meal, and to bring food with you to the exam.

      V. One's blood sugar levels can affect how clearly one is able to think and concentrate during an exam.

      A. V, IV, II, III, I   B. V, II, I, IV, III
      C. V, I, IV, III, II   D. V, IV, I, III, II

4.   I.   Those who are the embodiment of desire are absorbed in material quests, and those who are the embodiment of feeling are warriors who value power more than possession.   4.____

      II. These qualities are in everyone, but in different degrees.

      III. But those who value understanding yearn not for goods or victory, but for knowledge.

      IV. According to Plato, human behavior flows from three main sources: desire, emotion, and knowledge,

V. In the perfect state, the industrial forces would produce but not rule, the military would protect but not rule, and the forces of knowledge, the philosopher kings, would reign.

A. IV, V, I, II, III   B. V, I, II, III, IV
C. IV, III, II, I, V   D. IV, II, I, III, V

5.   I. Of the more than 26,000 tons of garbage produced daily in New York City, 12,000 tons arrive daily at Fresh Kills.
   II. In a month, enough garbage accumulates there to fill the Empire State Building.
  III. In 1937, the Supreme Court halted the practice of dumping the trash of New York City into the sea.
  IV. Although the garbage is compacted, in a few years the mounds of garbage at Fresh Kills will be the highest points south of Maine's Mount Desert Island on the Eastern Seaboard.
  V. Instead, tugboats now pull barges of much of the trash to Staten Island and the largest landfill in the world, Fresh Kills.

5.____

A. III, V, IV, I, II   B. III, V, II, IV, I
C. III, V, I, II, IV   D. III, II, V, IV, I

6.   I. Communists rank equality very high, but freedom very low.
   II. Unlike communists, conservatives place a high value on freedom and a very low value on equality.
  III. A recent study demonstrated that one way to classify people's political beliefs is to look at the importance placed on two words: freedom and equality.
  IV. Thus, by demonstrating how members of these groups feel about the two words, the study has proved to be useful for political analysts in several European countries.
  V. According to the study, socialists and liberals rank both freedom and equality very high, while fascists rate both very low.

6.____

A. III, V, I, II, IV   B. III, IV, V, I, II
C. III, V, IV, II, I   D. III, I, II, IV, V

7.   I. "Can there be anything more amazing than this?"
   II. If the riddle is successfully answered, his dead brothers will be brought back to life.
  III. "Even though man sees those around him dying every day," says Dharmaraj, "he still believes and acts as if he were immortal."
  IV. "What is the cause of ceaseless wonder?" asks the Lord of the Lake.
  V. In the ancient epic, The Mahabharata, a riddle is asked of one of the Pandava brothers.

7.____

A. V, II, I, IV, III   B. V, IV, III, I, II
C. V, II, IV, III, I   D. V, II, IV, I, III

8. I. On the contrary, the two main theories — the cooperative (neoclassical) theory and the radical (labor theory) — clearly rest on very different assumptions, which have very different ethical overtones.

II. The distribution of income is the primary factor in determining the relative levels of material well-being that different groups or individuals attain.

III. Of all issues in economics, the distribution of income is one of the most contro-versial.

IV. The neoclassical theory tends to support the existing income distribution (or minor changes), while the labor theory tends to support substantial changes in the way income is distributed.

V. The intensity of the controversy reflects the fact that different economic theories are not purely neutral, *detached* theories with no ethical or moral implications.

A. II, I, V, IV, III   B. III, II, V, I, IV
C. III, V, II, I, IV   D. III, V, IV, I, II

8.____

9. I. The pool acts as a broker and ensures that the cheapest power gets used first.
II. Every six seconds, the pool's computer monitors all of the generating stations in the state and decides which to ask for more power and which to cut back.
III. The buying and selling of electrical power is handled by the New York Power Pool in Guilderland, New York.
IV. This is to the advantage of both the buying and selling utilities.
V. The pool began operation in 1970, and consists of the state's eight electric utili-ties.

A. V, I, II, III, IV   B. IV, II, I, III, V
C. III, V, I, IV, II   D. V, III, IV, II, I

9.____

10. I. Modern English is much simpler grammatically than Old English.
II. Finnish grammar is very complicated; there are some fifteen cases, for example.
III. Chinese, a very old language, may seem to be the exception, but it is the great number of characters/ words that must be mastered that makes it so difficult to learn, not its grammar.
IV. The newest literary language — that is, written as well as spoken — is Finnish, whose literary roots go back only to about the middle of the nineteenth century.
V. Contrary to popular belief, the longer a language is been in use the simpler its grammar — not the reverse.

A. IV, I, II, III, V   B. V, I, IV, II, III
C. I, II, IV, III, V   D. IV, II, III, I, V

10.____

KEY (CORRECT ANSWERS)

1.	D	6.	A
2.	A	7.	C
3.	C	8.	B
4.	D	9.	C
5.	C	10.	B

TEST 2

DIRECTIONS: This type of question tests your ability to recognize accurate paraphrasing, well-constructed paragraphs, and appropriate style and tone. It is important that the answer you select contains only the facts or concepts given in the original sentences. It is also important that you be aware of incomplete sentences, inappropriate transitions, unsupported opinions, incorrect usage, and illogical sentence order. Paragraphs that do not include all the necessary facts and concepts, that distort them, or that add new ones are not considered correct.

The format for this section may vary. Sometimes, long paragraphs are given, and emphasis is placed on style and organization. Our first five questions are of this type. Other times, the paragraphs are shorter, and there is less emphasis on style and more emphasis on accurate representation of information. Our second group of five questions are of this nature.

For each of Questions 1 through 10, select the paragraph that BEST expresses the ideas contained in the sentences above it. *PRINT THE LETTER OF THE CORRECT ANSWER IN THE SPACE AT THE RIGHT.*

1. I.   Listening skills are very important for managers.   1.____
    II. Listening skills are not usually emphasized.
    III. Whenever managers are depicted in books, manuals or the media, they are always talking, never listening.
    IV. We'd like you to read the enclosed handout on listening skills and to try to consciously apply them this week.
    V.   We guarantee they will improve the quality of your interactions.

    A. Unfortunately, listening skills are not usually emphasized for managers. Managers are always depicted as talking, never listening. We'd like you to read the enclosed handout on listening skills. Please try to apply these principles this week. If you do, we guarantee they will improve the quality of your interactions.
    B. The enclosed handout on listening skills will be important improving the quality of your interactions. We guarantee it. All you have to do is take some time this week to read it and to consciously try to apply the principles. Listening skills are very important for managers, but they are not usually emphasized. Whenever managers are depicted in books, manuals or the media, they are always talking, never listening.
    C. Listening well is one of the most important skills a manager can have, yet it's not usually given much attention. Think about any representation of managers in books, manuals, or in the media that you may have seen. They're always talking, never listening. We'd like you to read the enclosed handout on listening skills and consciously try to apply them the rest of the week. We guarantee you will see a difference in the quality of your interactions.
    D. Effective listening, one very important tool in the effective manager's arsenal, is usually not emphasized enough. The usual depiction of managers in books, manuals or the media is one in which they are always talking, never listening. We'd like you to read the enclosed handout and consciously try to apply the information contained therein throughout the rest of the week. We feel sure that you will see a marked difference in the quality of your interactions.

2. I.   Chekhov wrote three dramatic masterpieces which share certain themes and formats: <u>Uncle Vanya</u>, <u>The Cherry Orchard</u>, and <u>The Three Sisters</u>.
    II. They are primarily concerned with the passage of time and how this erodes human aspirations.
    III. The plays are haunted by the ghosts of the wasted life.
    IV. The characters are concerned with life's lesser problems; however, such as the inability to make decisions, loyalty to the wrong cause, and the inability to be clear.
    V.   This results in a sweet, almost aching, type of a sadness referred to as Chekhovian.

    A.   Chekhov wrote three dramatic masterpieces: Uncle <u>Vanya</u>, <u>The Cherry Orchard,</u> and <u>The Three Sisters</u>. These masterpieces share certain themes and formats: the passage of time, how time erodes human aspirations, and the ghosts of wasted life. Each masterpiece is characterized by a sweet, almost aching, type of sadness that has become known as Chekhovian. The sweetness of this sadness hinges on the fact that it is not the great tragedies of life which are destroying these characters, but their minor flaws: indecisiveness, misplaced loyalty, unclarity.
    B.   <u>The Cherry Orchard</u>, <u>Uncle Vanya</u>, and <u>The Three Sisters</u> are three dramatic masterpieces written by Chekhov that use similar formats to explore a common theme. Each is primarily concerned with the way that passing time wears down human aspirations, and each is haunted by the ghosts of the wasted life. The characters are shown struggling futilely with the lesser problems of life: indecisiveness, loyalty to the wrong cause, and the inability to be clear. These struggles create a mood of sweet, almost aching, sadness that has become known as Chekhovian.
    C.   Chekhov's dramatic masterpieces are, along with <u>The Cherry Orchard</u>, <u>Uncle Vanya</u>, and The Three Sisters. These plays share certain thematic and formal similarities. They are concerned most of all with the passage of time and the way in which time erodes human aspirations. Each play is haunted by the specter of the wasted life. Chekhov's characters are caught, however, by life's lesser snares: indecisiveness, loyalty to the wrong cause, and unclarity. The characteristic mood is a sweet, almost aching type of sadness that has come to be known as Chekhovian.
    D.   A Chekhovian mood is characterized by sweet, almost aching, sadness. The term comes from three dramatic tragedies by Chekhov which revolve around the sadness of a wasted life. The three masterpieces (<u>Uncle Vanya</u>, <u>The Three Sisters</u>, and <u>The Cherry Orchard)</u> share the same theme and format. The plays are concerned with how the passage of time erodes human aspirations. They are peopled with characters who are struggling with life's lesser problems. These are people who are indecisive, loyal to the wrong causes, or are unable to make themselves clear.

3.   I. Movie previews have often helped producers decide what parts of movies they should take out or leave in.   3.____

    II. The first 1933 preview of <u>King Kong</u> was very helpful to the producers because many people ran screaming from the theater and would not return when four men first attacked by Kong were eaten by giant spiders.

    III. The 1950 premiere of Sunset Boulevard resulted in the filming of an entirely new beginning, and a delay of six months in the film's release.

    IV. In the original opening scene, William Holden was in a morgue talking with thirty-six other "corpses" about the ways some of them had died.

    V. When he began to tell them of his life with Gloria Swanson, the audience found this hilarious, instead of taking the scene seriously.

    A. Movie previews have often helped producers decide what parts of movies they should leave in or take out. For example, the first preview of <u>King Kong</u> in 1933 was very helpful. In one scene, four men were first attacked by Kong and then eaten by giant spiders. Many members of the audience ran screaming from the theater and would not return. The premiere of the 1950 film <u>Sunset Boulevard</u> was also very helpful. In the original opening scene, William Holden was in a morgue with thirty-six other "corpses," discussing the ways some of them had died. When he began to tell them of his life with Gloria Swanson, the audience found this hilarious. They were supposed to take the scene seriously. The result was a delay of six months in the release of the film while a new beginning was added.

    B. Movie previews have often helped producers decide whether they should change various parts of a movie. After the 1933 preview of <u>King Kong,</u> a scene in which four men who had been attacked by Kong were eaten by giant spiders was taken out as many people ran screaming from the theater and would not return. The 1950 premiere of <u>Sunset Boulevard</u> also led to some changes. In the original opening scene, William Holden was in a morgue talking with thirty-six other "corpses" about the ways some of them had died. When he began to tell them of his life with Gloria Swanson, the audience found this hilarious, instead of taking the scene seriously.

    C. What do <u>Sunset Boulevard</u> and <u>King Kong</u> have in common? Both show the value of using movie previews to test audience reaction. The first 1933 preview of <u>King Kong</u> showed that a scene showing four men being eaten by giant spiders after having been attacked by Kong was too frightening for many people. They ran screaming from the theater and couldn't be coaxed back. The 1950 premiere of <u>Sunset Boulevard </u>was also a scream, but not the kind the producers intended. The movie opens with William Holden lying in a morgue discussing the ways they had died with thirty-six other "corpses." When he began to tell them of his life with Gloria Swanson, the audience couldn't take him seriously. Their laughter caused a six-month delay while the beginning was rewritten.

    D. Producers very often use movie previews to decide if changes are needed. The premiere of <u>Sunset Boulevard </u>in 1950 led to a new beginning and a six-month delay in film release. At the beginning, William Holden and thirty-six other "corpses" discuss the ways some of them died. Rather than taking this seriously, the audience thought it was hilarious when he began to tell them of his life with Gloria Swanson. The first 1933 preview of <u>King Kong</u> was very helpful for its producers because one scene so terrified the audience that many of them ran screaming from the theater and would not return. In this particular scene, four men who had first been attacked by Kong were being eaten by giant spiders.

4.   I. It is common for supervisors to view employees as "things" to be manipulated.   4.____

    II. This approach does not motivate employees, nor does the carrot-and-stick approach because employees often recognize these behaviors and resent them.

    III. Supervisors can change these behaviors by using self-inquiry and persistence.

    IV. The best managers genuinely respect those they work with, are supportive and helpful, and are interested in working as a team with those they supervise.

    V. They disagree with the Golden Rule that says "he or she who has the gold makes the rules."

    A. Some managers act as if they think the Golden Rule means "he or she who has the gold makes the rules." They show disrespect to employees by seeing them as "things" to be manipulated. Obviously, this approach does not motivate employees any more than the carrot-and-stick approach motivates them. The employees are smart enough to spot these behaviors and resent them. On the other hand, the managers genuinely respect those they work with, are supportive and helpful, and are interested in working as a team. Self-inquiry and persistence can change even the former type of supervisor into the latter.

    B. Many supervisors fall into the trap of viewing employees as "things" to be manipulated, or try to motivate them by using a earrot-and-stick approach. These methods do not motivate employees, who often recognize the behaviors and resent them. Supervisors can change these behaviors, however, by using self-inquiry and persistence. The best managers are supportive and helpful, and have genuine respect for those with whom they work. They are interested in working as a team with those they supervise. To them, the Golden Rule is not "he or she who has the gold makes the rules."

    C. Some supervisors see employees as "things" to be used or manipulated using a carrot-and-stick technique. These methods don't work. Employees often see through them and resent them. A supervisor who wants to change may do so. The techniques of self-inquiry and persistence can be used to turn him or her into the type of supervisor who doesn't think the Golden Rule is "he or she who has the gold makes the rules." They may become like the best managers who treat those with whom they work with respect and give them help and support. These are the managers who know how to build a team.

    D. Unfortunately, many supervisors act as if their employees are objects whose movements they can position at will. This mistaken belief has the same result as another popular motivational technique—the carrot-and-stick approach. Both attitudes can lead to the same result — resentment from those employees who recognize the behaviors for what they are. Supervisors who recognize these behaviors can change through the use of persistence and the use of self-inquiry. It's important to remember that the best managers respect their employees. They readily give necessary help and support and are interested in working as a team with those they supervise. To these managers, the Golden Rule is not "he or she who has the gold makes the rules."

5.
  I. The first half of the nineteenth century produced a group of pessimistic poets —
     Byron, De Musset, Heine, Pushkin, and Leopardi.
  II. It also produced a group of pessimistic composers—Schubert, Chopin, Schumann, and even the later Beethoven.
  III. Above all, in philosophy, there was the profoundly pessimistic philosopher, Schopenhauer.
  IV. The Revolution was dead, the Bourbons were restored, the feudal barons were reclaiming their land, and progress everywhere was being suppressed, as the great age was over.
  V. "I thank God," said Goethe, "that I am not young in so thoroughly finished a world."

5.____

  A. "I thank God," said Goethe, "that I am not young in so thoroughly finished a world." The Revolution was dead, the Bourbons were restored, the feudal barons were reclaiming their land, and progress everywhere was being suppressed. The first half of the nineteenth century produced a group of pessimistic poets: Byron, De Musset, Heine, Pushkin, and Leopardi. It also produced pessimistic composers: Schubert, Chopin, Schumann. Although Beethoven came later, he fits into this group, too. Finally and above all, it also produced a profoundly pessimistic philosopher, Schopenhauer. The great age was over.
  B. The first half of the nineteenth century produced a group of pessimistic poets: Byron, De Musset, Heine, Pushkin, and Leopardi. It produced a group of pessimistic composers: Schubert, Chopin, Schumann, and even the later Beethoven. Above all, it produced a profoundly pessimistic philosopher, Schopenhauer. For each of these men, the great age was over. The Revolution was dead, and the Bourbons were restored. The feudal barons were reclaiming their land, and progress everywhere was being suppressed.
  C. The great age was over. The Revolution was dead—the Bourbons were restored, and the feudal barons were reclaiming their land. Progress everywhere was being suppressed. Out of this climate came a profound pessimism. Poets, like Byron, De Musset, Heine, Pushkin, and Leopardi; composers, like Schubert, Chopin, Schumann, and even the later Beethoven; and, above all, a profoundly pessimistic philosopher, Schopenauer. This pessimism which arose in the first half of the nineteenth century is illustrated by these words of Goethe, "I thank God that I am not young in so thoroughly finished a world."
  D. The first half of the nineteenth century produced a group of pessimistic poets, Byron, De Musset, Heine, Pushkin, and Leopardi — and a group of pessimistic composers, Schubert, Chopin, Schumann, and the later Beethoven. Above all, it produced a profoundly pessimistic philosopher, Schopenhauer. The great age was over. The Revolution was dead, the Bourbons were restored, the feudal barons were reclaiming their land, and progress everywhere was being suppressed. "I thank God," said Goethe, "that I am not young in so thoroughly finished a world."

6.
  I. A new manager sometimes may feel insecure about his or her competence in the new position.
  II. The new manager may then exhibit defensive or arrogant behavior towards those one supervises, or the new manager may direct overly flattering behavior toward one's new supervisor.

6.____

A. Sometimes, a new manager may feel insecure about his or her ability to perform well in this new position. The insecurity may lead him or her to treat others differently. He or she may display arrogant or defensive behavior towards those he or she supervises, or be overly flattering to his or her new supervisor.

B. A new manager may sometimes feel insecure about his or her ability to perform well in the new position. He or she may then become arrogant, defensive, or overly flattering towards those he or she works with.

C. There are times when a new manager may be insecure about how well he or she can perform in the new job. The new manager may also behave defensive or act in an arrogant way towards those he or she supervises, or overly flatter his or her boss.

D. Sometimes, a new manager may feel insecure about his or her ability to perform well in the new position. He or she may then display arrogant or defensive behavior towards those they supervise, or become overly flattering towards their supervisors.

7.   I.   It is possible to eliminate unwanted behavior by bringing it under stimulus control — tying the behavior to a cue, and then never, or rarely, giving the cue.   7.____

     II.   One trainer successfully used this method to keep an energetic young porpoise from coming out of her tank whenever she felt like it, which was potentially dangerous.

    III.   Her trainer taught her to do it for a reward, in response to a hand signal, and then rarely gave the signal.

A. Unwanted behavior can be eliminated by tying the behavior to a cue, and then never, or rarely, giving the cue. This is called stimulus control. One trainer was able to use this method to keep an energetic young porpoise from coming out of her tank by teaching her to come out for a reward in response to a hand signal, and then rarely giving the signal.

B. Stimulus control can be used to eliminate unwanted behavior. In this method, behavior is tied to a cue, and then the cue is rarely, if ever, given. One trainer was able to successfully use stimulus control to keep an energetic young porpoise from coming out of her tank whenever she felt like it — a potentially dangerous practice. She taught the porpoise to come out for a reward when she gave a hand signal, and then rarely gave the signal.

C. It is possible to eliminate behavior that is undesirable by bringing it under stimulus control by tying behavior to a signal, and then rarely giving the signal. One trainer successfully used this method to keep an energetic young porpoise from coming out of her tank, a potentially dangerous situation. Her trainer taught the porpoise to do it for a reward, in response to a hand signal, and then would rarely give the signal.

D. By using stimulus control, it is possible to eliminate unwanted behavior by tying the behavior to a cue, and then rarely or never give the cue. One trainer was able to use this method to successfully stop a young porpoise from coming out of her tank whenever she felt like it. To curb this potentially dangerous practice, the porpoise was taught by the trainer to come out of the tank for a reward, in response to a hand signal, and then rarely given the signal.

8. I.   There is a great deal of concern over the safety of commercial trucks, caused by   8.____
         their greatly increased role in serious accidents since federal deregulation in 1981.
    II. Recently, 60 percent of trucks in New York and Connecticut and 70 percent of
         trucks in Maryland randomly stopped by state troopers failed safety inspections.
    III. Sixteen states in the United States require no training at all for truck drivers.

    A.   Since federal deregulation in 1981, there has been a great deal of concern over the
         safety of commercial trucks, and their greatly increased role in serious accidents.
         Recently, 60 percent of trucks in New York and Connecticut, and 70 percent of
         trucks in Maryland failed safety inspections. Sixteen states in the United States
         require no training at all for truck drivers.
    B.   There is a great deal of concern over the safety of commercial trucks since federal
         deregulation in 1981. Their role in serious accidents has greatly increased.
         Recently, 60 percent of trucks randomly stopped in Connecticut and New York, and
         70 percent in Maryland failed safety inspections conducted by state troopers. Six-
         teen states in the United States provide no training at all for truck drivers.
    C.   Commercial trucks have a greatly increased role in serious accidents since federal
         deregulation in 1981. This has led to a great deal of concern. Recently, 70 percent
         of trucks in Maryland and 60 percent of trucks in New York and Connecticut failed
         inspection of those that were randomly stopped by state troopers. Sixteen states in
         the United States require no training for all truck drivers.
    D.   Since federal deregulation in 1981, the role that commercial trucks have played in
         serious accidents has greatly increased, and this has led to a great deal of con-
         cern. Recently, 60 percent of trucks in New York and Connecticut, and 70 percent
         of trucks in Maryland randomly stopped by state troopers failed safety inspections.
         Sixteen states in the U.S. don't require any training for truck drivers.

9. I.   No matter how much some people have, they still feel unsatisfied and want more,   9.____
         or want to keep what they have forever.
    II. One recent television documentary showed several people flying from New York
         to Paris for a one-day shopping spree to buy platinum earrings, because they
         were bored.
    III. In Brazil, some people are ordering coffins that cost a minimum of $45,000 and
         are equipping them with deluxe stereos, televisions and other graveyard neces-
         sities.

    A.   Some people, despite having a great deal, still feel unsatisfied and want more, or
         think they can keep what they have forever. One recent documentary on television
         showed several people enroute from Paris to New York for a one day shopping
         spree to buy platinum earrings, because they were bored. Some people in Brazil
         are even ordering coffins equipped with such graveyard necessities as deluxe ste-
         reos and televisions. The price of the coffins start at $45,000.
    B.   No matter how much some people have, they may feel unsatisfied. This leads them
         to want more, or to want to keep what they have forever. Recently, a television doc-
         umentary depicting several people flying from New York to Paris for a one day
         shopping spree to buy platinum earrings. They were bored. Some people in Brazil
         are ordering coffins that cost at least $45,000 and come equipped with deluxe tele-
         visions, stereos and other necessary graveyard items.
    C.   Some people will be dissatisfied no matter how much they have. They may want
         more, or they may want to keep what they have forever. One recent television doc-
         umentary showed several people, motivated by boredom, jetting from New York to

Paris for a one-day shopping spree to buy platinum earrings. In Brazil, some people are ordering coffins equipped with deluxe stereos, televisions and other graveyard necessities. The minimum price for these coffins - $45,000.

D. Some people are never satisfied. No matter how much they have they still want more, or think they can keep what they have forever. One television documentary recently showed several people flying from New York to Paris for the day to buy platinum earrings because they were bored. In Brazil, some people are ordering coffins that cost $45,000 and are equipped with deluxe stereos, televisions and other graveyard necessities.

10. I. A television signal or Video signal has three parts. 10.____
II. Its parts are the black-and-white portion, the color portion, and the synchronizing (sync) pulses, which keep the picture stable.
III. Each video source, whether it's a camera or a video-cassette recorder, contains its own generator of these synchronizing pulses to accompany the picture that it's sending in order to keep it steady and straight.
IV. In order to produce a clean recording, a video-cassette recorder must "lock-up" to the sync pulses that are part of the video it is trying to record, and this effort may be very noticeable if the device does not have genlock.

A. There are three parts to a television or video signal: the black-and-white part, the color part, and the synchronizing (sync) pulses, which keep the picture stable. Whether it's a video-cassette recorder or a camera, each each video source contains its own pulse that synchronizes and generates the picture it's sending in order to keep it straight and steady. A video-cassette recorder must "lock up" to the sync pulses that are part of the video it's trying to record. If the device doesn't have genlock, this effort must be very noticeable.

B. A video signal or television is comprised of three parts: the black-and-white portion, the color portion, and the the sync (synchronizing) pulses, which keep the picture stable. Whether it's a camera or a video-cassette recorder, each video source contains its own generator of these synchronizing pulses. These accompany the picture that it's sending in order to keep it straight and steady. A video-cassette recorder must "lock up" to the sync pulses that are part of the video it is trying to record in order to produce a clean recording. This effort may be very noticeable if the device does not have genlock.

C. There are three parts to a television or video signal: the color portion, the black-and-white portion, and the sync (synchronizing pulses). These keep the picture stable. Each video source, whether it's a video-cassette recorder or a camera, generates these synchronizing pulses accompanying the picture it's sending in order to keep it straight and steady. If a clean recording is to be produced, a video-cassette recorder must store the sync pulses that are part of the video it is trying to record. This effort may not be noticeable if the device does not have genlock.

D. A television signal or video signal has three parts: the black-and-white portion, the color portion, and the synchronizing (sync) pulses. It's the sync pulses which keep the picture stable, which accompany it and keep it steady and straight. Whether it's a camera or a video-cassette recorder, each video source contains its own generator of these synchronizing pulses. To produce a clean recording, a video-cassette recorder must "lock-up" to the sync pulses that are part of the video it is trying to record. If the device does not have genlock, this effort may be very noticeable.

___

KEY (CORRECT ANSWERS)

1.	C		6.	A
2.	B		7.	B
3.	A		8.	D
4.	B		9.	C
5.	D		10.	D

———

CPSIA information can be obtained
at www.ICGtesting.com
Printed in the USA
LVHW022054171219
640814LV00022B/506